PRAISE FOR THE LAST QUEST

"The Last Quest is a fantastic read about a life truth that applies to everyone and especially the business executives who are chasing their dream. Dr Senyard does a masterful job of weaving a story to everyday business. It is like Pilgrim's Progress meets McKinsey consulting. This story will greatly encourage and refocus your personal quest." Bruce Witt, President, Leadership Revolution.

"According to a recent survey of business owners that sold their businesses, 75% were unhappy after one year, primarily because their identity resided in their businesses, therefore leaving them without a purpose post-exit. In The Last Quest, Dr. Senyard brings a unique perspective of one owner's journey to discovering his true identity, preparing him for a purposeful and joyful next season of life." Scott Barth, Exit Planner and Value Acceleration Coach

"*The Last Quest* brings a fresh breeze to stagnant business books. Dr. Bill's uniquely inventive book will guide and focus your spirits and get you on course for your joyful professional life of meaning and contribution." Eric Protzman, Business Made Simple, Senior Business Growth Coach.

DR. BILL SENYARD

"*The Last Quest* is a great example that if you want to tell the truth, you write fiction. Dr. Senyard wrote exactly what I needed to help me refocus on what's important in my business. I was measuring my value and success through a world economy instead of through the economy of the Father's kingdom. The story within the story reminded me that I just need to be a good steward of what was never mine to begin with." Steve Bock, Founder and CEO, Subsentio.

The Last Quest

Business Exit Strategy From An Unlikely Source

Dr. Bill Senyard

Acknowledgements

I want to especially acknowledge four organizations for businesspersons that have not only inspired me but have also significantly contributed to the promotion of ethical business practices and Christian values for the common good and inspire many others to do the same.

The Christian Business Men's Connection: CBMC's stated mission is to "present Jesus Christ as Savior and Lord to business and professional men and to develop Christian business and professional men to carry out the Great Commission." (https://www.cbmc.com/)

C12: C12 helps CEOs and executives "calibrate the entirety of their businesses through its signature "5-Point Alignment Matrix," which includes encouraging every C12 member to view their business as a means to make a "Kingdom impact in the marketplace." (https://www.joinc12.com)

Convene: Convene's mission is to "connect, equip and inspire Christian CEOs and business owners to grow exceptional businesses and become higher-impact leaders to honor God." (https://www.convenenow.com)

Lastly, I have been active in several Rotary Clubs in the US and Canada. All members are encouraged to live by the time-tested Rotary Four Way Test of the things we think, say, or do.

> First, is it the TRUTH? Second, is it FAIR to all concerned? Third, will it build GOODWILL and BETTER FRIENDSHIPS? Fourth, will it be BENEFICIAL to all concerned?

May God bless and multiply each of you.

I would like to especially thank my beloved wife and editor, Eunice. Couldn't do it without you.

Contents

Prologue		XI
1.	Harvey the Entrepreneur	1
2.	The Last Quest	17
3.	The Tale of the Unlikely Prince	23
4.	Sarshalom's Choice	31
5.	The Making of a Great Coat of Arms	39
6.	The Prince's Problem	45
7.	Deeper Thoughts	53
8.	The Official Request	57
9.	The Great Quest Begins	63
10.	Harvey's Quest	73
11.	Can It Get Any Worse?	79
12.	The Others	89
13.	Kicking a Man Down	97
14.	The Beginning of the End	101
15.	The Beguiler	107

16.	The Shocking Question	117
17.	Not Always What They Appear	123
18.	Scooters Place	131
19.	T-Minus Five	143
20.	A Little Past Ouch	155
21.	Bo	167
22.	Ye Wee Scunner	173
23.	Sadie's Quest	183
24.	The Coffee Shop	187
25.	Finale: The Great King	199
26.	Dr. Ben	207
27.	And They All Lived Happily Ever After?	211
Enjoying This Book?		217
Also by Dr. Bill Senyard		218

Prologue

Here I must take counsel of the gospel. I must hearken to the gospel, which teaches me, not what I ought to do, (for that is the proper office of the law,) but what Jesus Christ the Son of God hath done for me: to wit, that He suffered and died to deliver me from sin and death. The gospel wills me to receive this, and to believe it. And this is the truth of the gospel. It is also the principal article of all Christian doctrine, wherein the knowledge of all godliness consists. Most necessary it is, therefore, that we should know this article well, teach it unto others, and beat it into their heads continually. —Martin Luther

"I'd rather be dead than sing 'Satisfaction' when I'm 45." — Mick Jagger, Rolling Stones (now 80 years old).

> "Say it, reader. Say the word 'quest' out loud. It is an extraordinary word, isn't it? So small and yet so full of wonder, so full of hope." —— Kate DiCamillo, *The Tale of Despereaux*

Business leader, I'm not telling you anything you don't know. Being a businessman or woman is difficult. To be successful over a long period, or for that matter, a whole career is something extraordinary and quite rare. Few women or men make it through unscathed and free from obvious scars.

Why? Challenges happen quickly in business: Supply chain disruptions, board revolts, corporate reorganizations, Chapter 11, hostile takeovers, pink slips, redirecting, walkouts, union negotiations, congressional investigations, downsizing, the vagaries of economic downturns, unpredictable interest rate hikes, irruption of pandemics, or AI—whatever that will turn out to be. These issues often feel like drive-by-shootings, each one creating new difficulties for real people at real desks where personalized nameplates proclaiming "The Buck Stops Here" tremble, hoping never to be needed. And none of it is your fault, not really.

When I was a strategic management consultant in the mid-80s, a very turbulent economic time, I was part of teams hired by Fortune 500 companies to help them 'minimize contingencies'—meaning, "We know the floods are coming, but we don't know where or when. Can you help us design lifeboats to save as many as we can?" Sometimes, the answer was 'yes' and sometimes 'no.'

You've probably heard these inspirational business quotes. You may even have them framed on the wall facing your desk. Perhaps they served you well in the minor career dips and valleys? But not when that iceberg rips through your professional hull.

- "Never dream for success but work for it."

- "When the Vision is clear, strategy is easy."

- "Old ways won't open New doors."

- "Work until you no longer have to introduce yourself."

- "When it rains, look for rainbows. When it's dark, look for a star."

Even now, they bring tears to my eyes, but not for the reason you might think.

You know as well as I do that there are times when such truisms are ridiculously shallow. They mock you and exacerbate your feelings of helplessness. Who wrote them anyway? Some summer intern at some 3x3 sq ft cubicle at Hallmark? Certainly not someone who has been through what you are going through. I am reminded of boxer Mike Tyson's response when asked by a reporter whether he was worried about Evander Holyfield and his fight plan. He answered, "Everyone has a plan until they get punched in the mouth."

For so many businessmen and women, there is no bigger punch in the mouth than the experience of retirement, planned or forced. The only thing harder than being a businessperson is to *stop* being a businessperson—to end your career, retire, divest, sell the business, get that golden handshake, leave the gun, take the cannoli (Godfather), call it a day, hang up your spurs, shut it all down, all so that you can finally work that floundering handicap down a couple of strokes. For many, that gets old quickly.

Why? After working for 60-80 hours a week for 50+ years, and finding most of your significance, security, and belonging in your bottom line, with people looking up to you, or at least fearing you a little bit, you now must shift to the vagaries of finding an age-appropriate pickleball league before you have to get a knee replacement.

For many career businessmen and women, retirement isn't what they hoped it might be. Did you know that one in three retirees say they feel depressed?

> "Retirement blues are a dirty secret," says Robert Delamontagne, PhD, author of *The Retiring Mind*. "People would ask me, 'How's retirement?' I used to say, 'It's great! I'm having a great time!' What was I supposed to say?" Leaving work can strip away your sense of purpose and self-worth. No longer do you reap the financial rewards and achievements that a job provides. The end of your daily routine can make you feel lost."[1]

Many people who have left the C-suite feel withdrawal symptoms, much like addicts. There is a void, a lack of direction, ego hits, identity issues, boredom, anxiety, and feelings of powerless-

---

1. https://www.webmd.com/healthy-aging/features/emotional-shock-retirement. Accessed October, 8, 2024.

ness. "Chairman of the board doesn't mean a thing when you're retired," says Delamontagne.

Then, relational adjustments must be made. You've heard the old saying, "I married you for better or worse, but not for breakfast, lunch, and dinner." One person has labeled the stressful phenomenon, 'marital compression.' You get the idea.

Then your financial advisor reminds you of the retirement Rule of Thumb, "You should have 25x your current gross income—that is, earnings before taxes and other deductions." Damn!

Don't mention all the usual human second-guessing—no judgment from me.

Was it all worth it?

I should have been a tuba player.

Could I have been a better father/mother, wife/husband, neighbor?

What legacy am I leaving to those who follow me?

Am I loved?

Have I loved?

Could I have made different decisions?

Am I fulfilled? Happy?

Did I change the world?

What does God think of me? Jesus? The Spirit?

Am I right?

Business leader, this book is not about new techniques for running your business more cost-effectively, sweating the details more, or having better professional relationships. All those things are good, and much has been written about them elsewhere.

The goal of this book is more foundational to your ultimate personal sense of enoughness and connectedness. Your career does not determine your well-being and worth—good or bad. Somewhere in the swirling shadows of your midbrain, you know this.

Could this capture the longing?

> "Let me explain it to you, let me run it down just briefly if I can. We're looking for the American Dream, and we were told it was somewhere in this area. Well, we're here looking for it, 'cause they sent us out here all the way from San Francisco to look for it. That's why they gave us this white Cadillac, they figure that we could catch up with it in that ..." Hunter S. Thompson, Fear and Loathing In Las Vegas

Did they catch up? Nope. This is true whether you are a business leader, president, owner, manager, or entrepreneur, whether you are C-Suite or living out of the alleyway on C-Street. This book is a fun, shame-free wake-up call for some of our world's best and brightest, most committed people—good news for you businesswomen and men.

The Last Quest is a fictional story about Harvey, a successful entrepreneur and businessman who is about to find all his hard work and effort disintegrating into nothingness and void. It's not his fault. He is a good man and a Christian, but neither seems to make any difference right now that he has been smashed in the mouth big time.

Seemingly by coincidence, he stumbles upon a tiny book for teens on his absent wife's nightstand, a young adult fantasy about dragons and quests. It is a fun, quirky, and an adventurous book about an insecure teenage prince who demands that the King send him on a special quest—no, an amazing, great quest, one like none other before or since. On that quest, both the prince and Harvey (hopefully) will learn that not all quests are the same and that this King is not what he seems.

It is in and through that short book that Harvey might find something significant, even if he didn't know it was missing or that he was looking for something—in all the wrong places. Curious?

Would you be willing to join Harvey on his life quest? You, too, may be surprised. What could it hurt?

Christian business leader, female or male, your life has been a series of quests. Now as you enter or are already in retirement, you are on your *Final Quest*. The characters of this book are all fictional, yet in a strange and fun way, I know every one of them. They each desperately need significance, security, and belonging—just like me—just like you. Welcome to the *Final Quest*!

1

HARVEY THE ENTREPRENEUR

"They say it is the first step that costs the effort. I do not find it so. I am sure I could write unlimited 'first chapters'. I have indeed written many."
——J.R.R. Tolkien

"Not all those who wander are lost."—— J.R.R. Tolkien

"Team, everyone needs to step up right now," Harvey snapped. He would not be misunderstood or have his words discounted. Not today.

"Everyone, including me, needs to be at the top of our game for the foreseeable future. Understand?" He looked around the table, making brief eye contact with each person. It made things very uncomfortable, to be sure. This was not like the old Harvey everybody loved.

His leadership team surrounded him at the large conference table. This meeting was not the regularly scheduled Tuesday morning forum. This was 4:40 on a Monday afternoon. The urgent text to the core managers read, "Conference room, 15 minutes. No excuses."

Harvey dramatically entered the room. He was wearing his typical white button-down shirt with sleeves rolled up, rumpled slacks, and reading glasses tied around his neck. Unceremoniously, he tossed a thick pile of disheveled papers in front of his chair at the business end of the large table. No one spoke. This was Harvey's company, clearly Harvey's meeting.

After an uncharacteristically long time, he finally began to speak. Harvey's brow furrowed, his voice urgent, his words unrehearsed, and his body language clear. Harvey was worried. He rubbed his thick hands through his sparse white hair, ungracefully shoved his third pair of Wal-Mart reading glasses this week onto his face, and looked down at a red-marked, drenched spreadsheet splayed before him.

Hunched forward, Harvey looked tired.

Harvey *was* very tired.

"People, you probably know…" He paused, shaking his head slowly, and let his reading glasses fall to his chest. "Of course, you do." He paused again, looking down dejectedly. "This recession is killing us. I am not blaming anyone. Maybe I am. I probably should have seen this coming. But I didn't. This is on me."

"We just need to work harder and smarter," he said, not looking at anyone in particular. "And someone needs to pull a rabbit out of their…uh—hat—or anywhere else, soon."

Sadie, short for Sandra, was very concerned for Harvey and had been for some time. She had been by his side from the beginning—back when they worked out of his small garage. He would bring in sales, and she would do the rest: everything from purchasing to manufacturing, bookkeeping, and coffee, yes, even rodent control.

Back then, it was exciting. Harvey was a savant, an entrepreneurial genius. Everything he touched seemed to turn to gold. Investors lined up to get a piece of Harvey's knack for the bottom line. His current company had found a sizable niche in the industry, and early on, they had difficulty keeping up with orders.

The company quickly grew from Harvey's garage to a small rental unit, and now it has a large warehouse with sixty employees. Sadie oversaw all manufacturing, from ordering to shipping, and did it well. However, she was not a miracle worker and had no power over an entire economy turning south.

Sadie looked at Harvey with motherly endearment. She knew he couldn't keep this up much longer. What little hair he had left was white and unkempt. His eyes were uncharacteristically puffy. Years ago, they had both talked about retiring in their mid-60s. Harvey was 69 last June, and Sadie was, well, let's just say, not middle-aged anymore, either. There appeared to be no apparent exit strategy. Most of Harvey's best friends had retired, died, or checked into homes. Would her friend and mentor be far behind?

She wondered if he was still taking Percocet for his back. She knew of others like him who had lived with high stress and got hooked on pain meds. Harvey swore he had stopped but didn't want to discuss it further. She wasn't so sure. He was guarding his back.

He hadn't golfed for weeks. Not only was golf a vital outlet for his stress, but he also loved his foursome buddies almost as much as he liked creating businesses. They understood him, he thought. But everything was falling apart.

Ron, his best friend, had been a manager at Goldman Sachs until a few months ago. His wife found him slumped over in his favorite chair in his thirty thousand-dollar, recently remodeled man cave. It was a severe stroke, not unexpected. His blood pressure was way above what the doctor wanted. He drank himself to sleep almost every night—15-year-aged GlenDronach Single Malt—and smoked one of his favorite cigars, the Davidoff white label Double, a classic corona from the Dominican Republic. It was wrapped in an oily Ecuadorian Habano wrapper. Ron enjoyed the dark chocolate and coffee notes, but he actually liked the fat, stubby Corona feel—it made him feel "gangsta," he said with a grin. The cigar shop owner ordered them specifically for Ron. A whole box costs just under $1000.

"How can someone like Ron be replaced?" Harvey went into a dark funk for weeks. "Is this all there is?"

That reminded Harvey of another tragedy. Another golfing buddy, Robert, a very successful young banker, had gone cave diving with a group off the coast of Florida. He was younger, in his early 60s, and in pretty good shape, all things considered. Something went wrong. A rescue team was sent in after the group failed to appear at the designated rendezvous spot before their air was calculated to run out. When they found their bodies, none of them had made it. On his diver's portable blackboard, Robert wrote, "Is this all there is?" No one knew if he was referring to oxygen remaining in their tanks or life in general.

It had been a difficult twelve months.

Anyway, there was no time for golf now. Harvey's company was tanking.

The $8 million high revenue mark they had hit in 2017 had been shattered. They were looking at $3 million at the end of this year, closer to $2 million. Pink slips had gone out last month to a dozen employees, a couple of whom had been with the company for over a decade. These people were like family.

But what else could be done? The recent months had been hard on everyone, including Sadie. The late nights and pressure were also taking a toll on her home life. Her husband, a philosophy and religion professor at a local university, told her he had enough of the stress that she would bring home. She knew he was right. But...

"Sadie," Harvey said in a quiet, desperate tone, "can anything more be done to reduce costs? We need to make more adjustments to..."

"You mean fire more people, don't you, Harvey?" She shot back, her curtness surprising even herself. "Why not say what you mean?"

Sadie realized she was being louder than her usual soft-spoken tone—and angrier. Harvey's eyes jerked up toward her. Her words had wounded him. She had to admit that she felt both sad and righteous at the same time.

There was more awkward silence at the table. Harvey subconsciously glanced at the framed Rotary Four-Way Test hanging on the back wall across from him. He knew them by heart, and they had guided him through many rough waters. "The Four-Way Test of the things we think, say, or do. First, Is it the TRUTH? Second, Is it FAIR to all concerned? Third, Will it build GOODWILL and BETTER FRIENDSHIPS? Fourth, Will it be BENEFICIAL to all concerned?" Today, he felt they only mocked him. Such was the state of his mind.

"Yes, I suppose you are right—as always," Harvey said, this time even more dejectedly. "That is exactly what I mean."

Harvey didn't challenge her, not this time. His voice was now quiet, reserved, and without any emotion. "I don't know what choice we have."

Sadie looked straight at him, frustrated and tired. She threw her hands in the air and exclaimed, "What's going on, Harvey? Are we going to make it? What do I tell the staff?"

This was not Harvey's first rodeo. He started and sold three other businesses before this one. He knew tough economies before; there were downturns in 1991 and 2001. Harvey confidently—almost magically—rode through those recessions and won. He was like a champion bull rider—no fear, no hesitation—nothing stopped him until now.

In 2003, he sold the rest of his companies and invested all his savings, energies, and reputation into this venture. This economic downturn was taking it all.

Harvey was approaching the panic stage, though he didn't allow himself to admit it even privately.

He shook his head and looked down at the table. "Only God knows," Harvey said in answer to her question. He didn't mean it in any religious way. He was just being frank. "I don't."

Unfortunately, Dwayne raised his hand to speak. Sadie tried to stop him, but it was too late. This would not go well.

Dwayne, the young, bearded, skinny jeans-wearing Millennial generation caricature who had just last spring earned his MBA with a minor in psychology from the local university, unfortunately for all, took this opportunity to speak up.

By appearance, Dwayne was a strange combination of Buddy Holly and Justin Bieber. As an intern, he was minimally two and a half decades younger than the next oldest manager on the team. Dwayne was very bright and liked to remind people often—140 IQ, graduating near the top of his class. He explained to more than one person that he would have been at the very top of his class except for coming down with the flu during exam week. What he had in IQ, he lacked in EQ.

Unfortunately, he took this opportunity to share his 140 IQ with the rest of the table, a virtual brain dump. It couldn't be described any other way than a lecture—hard for the others to tell if he was well-meaning or demeaning, indeed not a poster child for humility.

"Look, I'm sorry," unknowingly channeling his inner Bieber. ("You gotta go and get angry at all my honesty, sorry")—and clearly, not sorry at all.

"I'm the new guy here, but I have been talking to many people, including a bunch of our customers, who are scared about the company's direction. They told me..." pausing for effect and tenting his fingers to appear more guru-esque. "They *all* told me they were planning on going to our competitors...totally. You know. They asked me why we don't have more social media presence and some tech support younger than fifty. No judgment. We just aren't listening to the customers. Like, I am sorry if this offends anyone, you know, but it is the truth. Better said now than after the ship sinks."

Among Dwayne's many gifts was the ability to use the truth to distribute blame to as many people in authority as possible—never himself. That would require being in a role with any authority. With such an imposing brain, one would think he would have a better grasp on timing and context. This ill-timed and insensitive browbeating was beyond inappropriate. It felt like a rusty jailhouse shiv to Harvey.

Harvey slammed his hands on the table and yelled, "Enough!" His face reddened, and his jaws clenched, "Anyone else who wants to take a shot at running this company like our young Einstein here? Hmmm? Aaron? Meg? Sebastian? Anyone?"

He paused and looked into each person's eyes for effect. "I didn't think so. Dwayne, let me see if I heard you. You have been talking to *all* our customers about the failings of *my* company? In fact, you have found that 'lots of them' agree with you. Am I listening well enough?" Harvey emphasized 'listening' as he stared into Dwayne's shocked face.

From the looks of it, Dwayne still couldn't see just how undermining his words were, particularly if he had been having such conversations with the company's customers behind the company's back.

"Well," added Harvey, clapping his hands. "The pupil has eclipsed the master. It looks like we have no more to teach you, Big D. You have mastered my business in a record-breaking six short months. If I had all the answers like you, I wouldn't hang around a sinking ship like this either. I would go out and start my own flawless company. Congratulations! Your internship is officially over. Go pack up your things. You are done here. And...oh, yeah...sorry!"

If the room wasn't tense before, it certainly was now. This was not Harvey—not the Harvey they knew. Harvey had always been kind and soft-spoken, like a father to them. He was their leader, an entrepreneur, and a bit invincible—always with a card or two up his sleeve.

Sadie remembered, but this wasn't the time to remind him; it was Harvey who brought Dwayne on staff, a new management intern position, preaching to the team that we need to lift the next generation—get them on board. Frankly, he had been the only one patient with Dwayne's millennialism. But no more.

Harvey worked until 9:45 that night, like most evenings. He put on his old jacket, wearily got in his 2014 Ford F150, and drove to his comfortable executive home nestled on the 8th hole of the Tiger Wood's designed golf course in an upscale gated community, about thirty-five minutes from the plant. He used to play golf two or three times a week, but then Ron and Jim died, and his back started acting up again. Sad.

His wife was away—again—visiting her older sister who had just gone into hospice with third-stage breast cancer. He probably should have gone with her, but he had responsibilities. This was not a good time for him to take off. She wanted to go alone anyway.

They belonged to an old, established church in the community. He would describe himself as a 'good Christian.' But he had grown less and less in sync with his church and organized religion. Maybe the right word is just 'bored.' First and foremost, he was a businessman. Religion had its place, but the world ran on profits. He recently had that conversation with Peter, one of his few remaining golf buddies, a fellow Rotarian, and a man on the church's board of directors this term.

Over a beer, Peter asked Harvey about God, church, and other things. Harvey took a deep draught of the pale ale made by a local craft brewery and complained, "I like to separate God from my bottom line. You know what I mean. Where was God when I needed him in 2001 or '08?"

Peter and Harvey had gone through catechism together decades ago. Harvey didn't remember much about the topics anymore. He was a member of the church and was "in good standing." That was sufficient. It's not like he was going to teach Sunday school anytime soon.

"Look, I've been a good man," Harvey said slightly too defensively. "I gave to a lot of charities. I was one of the founders and board members of the local food bank. If anyone could make it to heaven with his head held high, it would be me. Right? What else does God require of me? Maybe He won't say, 'Well done, good and faithful servant!' I mean...I am not a missionary or a minister. But I have given a lot. Just ask Pastor Rick. He'll tell you. I have been faithful to my wife. None of my kids did drugs or anything else kids do today. I am a good man."

If the truth were known, Harvey *was* a good man—no arguments there. Yet, he had grown increasingly distant from the church and maybe from God. The worship service didn't draw his interest as much as it used to when he was younger. It all seemed less relevant to his life somehow.

Deep down, he didn't expect much from church, worship, prayer, or, for that matter, God anymore. He was a businessman.

His reputation and security were dependent on his talents and efforts. Right?

"God? He has His priorities in the world. I leave Him alone, and He leaves me alone. I am not perfect. I have made mistakes, but the good I have done far outweighs all the bad—you can be sure."

Eleanor, Harvey's wife, was concerned for him, but they didn't have the kind of relationship where she could speak about spiritual matters. Pastor Rick regularly asked Eleanor how Harvey was doing and said he was praying for him, but he didn't mention any specific prayer requests. What could he say that might make a difference?

Pastor Rick, though, had noticed a disturbing trend. Harvey was one of many professionals, men and women, who were once dynamic church leaders but participated less and less as they aged. The things of the church didn't seem to interest them as they once did. Religion and faith were less relevant than making decisions critical to the lives of so many at their companies.

Harvey saw his role as a faithful tither to the church which was set up for monthly direct deposit. He wanted to do the right thing—even be generous. Of course, the board was appreciative and said so to Harvey and Eleanor.

Having said that, any objective observer would note that the relationship was on the decline. Harvey was one of many aging Boomers who were less involved in their church, having little excitement and few expectations of any real change.

Harvey heated the leftover casserole Eleanor left in the refrigerator for him and sat down to eat in front of his favorite news show on his sizeable 65-inch TV. He poured himself a glass of Wild Turkey 101. It wasn't GlenDronach single malt, but it worked for Harvey.

He held the glass up to the light. He always thought the light shining through the caramel liquid and ice was beautiful—even addictive. Then, there was the musical tinkling of ice in the tumbler. He could understand how some became alcoholics. Harvey remembered his dad's favorite being Wild Turkey 101, too. Every night, his dad would drink a glass straight up. Harvey knew when Dad sat down with his full tumbler, he was to be left alone. It's funny what you remember.

Harvey was never really close with his dad. He was only a young boy when his dad, Sam, died in a fatal car accident. His mother never said too much about it, but Harvey suspected alcohol was involved.

Harvey suspected the bigger problem was that his dad's once thriving business was about to go bankrupt—a combination of bad business decisions, a bad economy, and plain old foolish pride. It happens.

Even though Harvey was young at the time, he remembered his dad drinking more and more. He wouldn't let anyone help him. Sam was a very proud man. That's how men were back then. Show no weakness. Keep everything inside. Talk about it? No way!

The drinking became so bad that his mother would pack up the two boys to spend a few days at her sister's across town. She called it a vacation, but the boys knew it had something to do with Dad and his drinking. Then they received word his dad had died. He had driven right into a bridge barrier—instant death. Car totaled. The police said fog was involved. Maybe. Nobody talked about it, but Harvey's brother Sam Jr. believed it was suicide—"death by shame," he called it. This was Dad retaking charge of his life—or his death. He didn't need help.

Mom got a fat check from the insurance company days before the business went Chapter 11. In the end, Dad was a provider, at least income-wise—not so much for relationships. Harvey wondered how his life would have been different if his dad had lived longer. Probably not much, he concluded.

Sam wasn't very vocal about his feelings or praise for the boys. Harvey couldn't remember his dad ever hugging him. He was sure his dad never said, "Harvey, do you know how much I love you?" That's OK. Men must be strong, and needing others is a weakness.

A couple of marriage counselors back, Harvey was told he was still looking for his dad's approval. That's why he was so determined to make businesses work, spend so much time there, stress over the bottom line, and spend little time at home. The counselor suggested Harvey felt he needed to be more successful than his father to prove he was a worthy son. Then his dad wouldn't leave him. He would tell him how proud of him he was, hug him and say how much he loved him.

"Oh yeah," one shrink asked snarkily, "What was your dad's alcohol of choice?"

"That's ridiculous!" Harvey blurted out defensively. "Pure crap. I didn't really have a father. If I did, I certainly have no feelings toward him now. He didn't care enough for us to stick around. That's on him, not me! I am an orphan. What I have done, I have done on my own. I don't need him to tell me he was proud."

Harvey sat motionless on the couch as his mind drew precariously close to the same dark rabbit hole. Harvey looked down at his drink, lifted it to his lips, and chugged it. He hadn't thought of his brother, Sam Jr., for a long time.

"How long ago was it?" He tried to remember. "At least a decade. No, more than that."

Sam Jr. had fallen from a ladder and hurt his back severely. After a week of rehab, he came home and, a couple of days later, went back to work, but he was never the same. Cynthia, his wife, said he would never talk about his pain, but it was clearly there. "Sharing feelings," said Sam Jr., "is a weakness and not my thing." Sam Jr. was just like the old man.

Weeks passed, and Sam became more distant and isolated. Harvey came running when he got the call from Cynthia. "Harvey, your brother is in the hospital. He's not going to make it much longer." Harvey couldn't believe what he saw when he went into the hospital room. Sam's lips were blue, his skin clammy, and he couldn't stop shaking. They now know he had become addicted to painkillers and had overdosed on a nasty combination of oxycontin and alcohol. There was little the doctor could do. Sam Jr. died alone, surrounded by his family.

Harvey poured himself another glass.

"Well, the good thing is Sam Jr.'s pain is over—no more shame. He doesn't have to cover up anymore. He doesn't have to deal with the failures in his life. He's free."

What shocked Harvey was the voice in his head wasn't his. It was his dad's.

What a thought. This evening, it became as clear as could be to Harvey. "That's the big deal, right?" He hadn't felt free for a long time. Certainly not now. It's done for his dad and brother. But he's more than likely suffering failure once again—being exposed as a lousy provider—possibly ending his life exposed as a bad husband and businessman—just like dad—just like Sam Jr.

"What is it with my family?" he declared.

It's true. Harvey's first marriage had ended in a very public explosion, expensive lawyers, and his children taken by her. But he did what men do and muscled through it. He had hoped to stay in touch with his two boys, but it just didn't work out, and now, well...."

His current marriage was better—at least it was at the start. But he and Eleanor kind of let things go a bit—maybe a lot? Counseling was her idea, and it seemed to only make matters worse. She said Harvey was distant and closed off. "She just doesn't understand," he thought to himself. Or did he say it aloud? He couldn't be sure. More darkness.

This was his third business venture. The previous two had success at first, but both ran out of runway. Both were also very public failures, with Harvey firing many friends who had trusted him. It was the hardest thing he had ever done, and he still couldn't look some of them or their spouses in the eyes. He knew they felt betrayed, but what could Harvey do? It was just business. He tried to rehire some when he got his next venture going, but it wasn't the same.

"I don't think I can do it again. God no!" He said as he took another slug. He was young then and had a lot more energy than now. Maybe he was a better businessman. Maybe he just cared more then. Now, he is tired, and his back hurts.

He takes painkillers for his back, too, just like Sam Jr., but he tells himself that he is careful not to lose control. Lesson learned from Sam Jr. The oxycontin helps, but he still doesn't sleep well, which makes matters worse. He tosses and turns most nights.

Like most evenings lately, Harvey is downing a very heady cocktail made up of Turkey 101. His chronic pain is minimally managed by oxy; he has fears of being a failure again, and of course, he is alone. Maybe it's the booze speaking, but right now, on this couch, he wonders if he can survive this one or if he wants to. It is his choice, after all. He is his father's son. He is Sam Jr.'s brother.

As if awakened from a dream state, Harvey jerked his head and mumbled as he fell into a shallow sleep, "Harvey, Harvey, Harvey, this isn't you. You are not your father or your brother. You are better than that."

Tonight, it seems Harvey will dodge another bullet—maybe. An objective observer would note that these downward emotional slopes happen more often. But for Harvey, there are no objective observers. He will not let his wife get too close. He is very adept at denial. It is accurate to say he is a train wreck about to happen. Will it be days, weeks, or months? Can't say for sure. But something must happen soon. Harvey, the good man, the gifted entrepreneur, self-sufficient, and distant husband, the Christian, is depressed. More to the point, he is alone.

2

The Last Quest

Harvey woke with a jerk, dropping his plate of unfinished casserole onto the faux-Persian rug his wife had purchased to "bring some warmth to the TV room." He had slept for a while and woke up in the middle of the Tonight Show. He could only take 15 minutes of the new host's sense of humor anyway. "I can remember the days of Johnny Carson and Ed McMahon. Now that was real entertainment! Not this schlock," Harvey muttered as he massaged the crick in his neck from slouching in the wrong position for so long. "Probably what woke me up," he thought.

He picked up what lumps of casserole he could with his hands and went to get a sponge for the rest. "Hard to tell," he thought. The worst spill fell among a darker pattern. It would hardly be noticeable to his wife. Oh, who was he kidding?

He finally finished cleaning up the mess and turned the TV off.

"Well, a couple of hours of sleep. I guess that's a win!"

Usually, he read for an hour or so. It helped him forget his back pain a bit. Pain Management 101, he called it.

He currently enjoyed Patterson novels. They are easy to read and distract him from the stresses of the day. The good thing about

Patterson's books was that they were much easier to process than real life. "Just what the doctor ordered," he thought.

As he was about to get ready for bed, he just happened to look at the stand to his right at the side of the overstuffed, earth-green sofa. El's reading glasses rested on top of what looked like a young adult fantasy book. Interesting. From the cover, it looked like a knock-off Harry Potter adventure.

He wasn't clear on what was more peculiar—El reading a fantasy book for teenagers or him noticing. Curiosity got the best of him, and he carefully reached over, moved her glasses aside, and picked up the book. It was his house, and he had earned the right to snoop.

"*Tale of the Unlikely Prince*, cheesy title," he thought. It wasn't clear if it was a kid's book, but it had princes, quests, and dragons. However, it had a soft cover—it could have been a Patterson novel, just shorter.

He leaned back and remembered tales of chivalry and knights as a boy. He had wanted to be a great prince, respected, honored, the conqueror of great quests.

The cover was quite well done, he thought, engaging—and fun. He flipped to chapter one and discovered the royal coat of arms. All quests need a royal coat of arms, right? "Let's see," he thought. He used to be good at reading coat of arms.

The coat of arms was a tri-part royal blue shield beneath a regal rampant lion with a red tongue and fierce claws. The lion was standing on top of a dragon beneath his paws.

He needed El's glasses to make out the words. In the upper left third of the shield was written "*Mishpat*" on top of judicial scales. The similarly mysterious word "*Tzedakah*" was in the upper right on top of a red heart. In the bottom third section was the phrase "*Lipnay Melek*" scripted above a portrayal of a mother gazing into the eyes of her infant. He wondered if it was Latin—maybe not. He would have to look those words up when he got to his computer. Google would know for sure.

Harv thought the image on the cover might be a little too scary for young adolescents. However, he reasoned, "I guess kids today are kind of used to lots of violence."

He had to smile, or at least he thought he smiled. He is no longer sure if he smiles outwardly or not. It had been a while since he felt like a carefree boy. This was a nice feeling. Maybe he would check out the first chapter—at least to find out what the coat of arms represented.

He would carefully put it back under El's glasses so she would never know. That might lead to a conversation he didn't need or want now. "But she's not here and will never find out. Right?" He asked himself.

Without thinking, he turned the book over to read the back cover. Harvey always reads the back cover first. It's only appropriate due diligence. Books have an agenda.

The scroll across the top said, "20th week on the New York Times fiction best-seller list." Surprisingly, the author, Ben McClellan, was the professor of religious studies and humanities at the same local university where Sadie's husband taught philosophy—most likely in the same humanities department. Dr. McClellan's credentials, including other award-winning books, were impressive, even for a skeptic like Harvey. He read the introduction with growing intrigue:

> "The Quest? All religions, and for that matter, all humanity's quests are for three things and only three

things. They go by many names and many descriptions. There are abundant counterfeits, yet only three core drivers for all decisions, all successes, all failures—in a word, all quests. Best-selling Author Ben McClellan suggests that all of life is a quest, consciously or subconsciously, for these three things: *significance, security,* and *belonging.* All great and lasting tales are written about them, yet they are never the lead characters. All great ventures and businesses are launched because their products and services inspire in their employees these three things and satisfy their customers' longings for these three things. The advertising world understands this perfectly. Wars are fought over them. Religions rise and wane over them. Societies, philosophies, and lifestyles fulcrum on this triad."

"So, your life and mine also revolve around such a quest for these three things, whether you know it or not. Intrigued? Join the quest—the Last Quest. Or, to put it another way, come and reimagine the quest you are already on."

Harvey's eyes arched, and his curiosity piqued. He turned to the first page right after the title. It was a disclaimer. Very smart, he thought.

No dragons, elves, or gnomes were physically harmed in the writing of this book. A few got their feelings hurt by the alleged negative representations included. It turns out many dragons are very sensitive. Who knew? We regret any discomfort caused by the story. Also, all dragons appearing in this work are fictitious. Any resemblance to real dragons, living or dead, is purely coincidental.

He thought this could be fun, and he needed a diversion. This was it. The Wild Turkey 101 was starting to do its thing, and he was beginning to relax. What could it hurt?

3

THE TALE OF THE UNLIKELY PRINCE

"No book is really worth reading at the age of 10 which is not equally – and often far more - worth reading at the age of fifty and beyond." C.S. Lewis

With some enthusiasm and interest that he hadn't remembered feeling in a long time, Harvey opened the colorful cover and turned to chapter one of *Tale of the Unlikely Prince* and began to read:

"There are tales we tell our children when they go to bed," began the storyteller with a wave of her hand, hushing the large audience before her. "Then there are stories we adults read for instruction, fun, and inspiration—motivating us through our hard days. But few true legends not only entertain generation after generation but also shape a people, a culture and even a world. Hear one such account."

The storyteller paused and graciously looked about the room into the engaged eyes of person after person, the tall, the short, the large, the small, the men, women, boys, girls, the well-off and the poor, light-skinned, dark-skinned—all who had gathered for this extraordinary event.

The grand royal stage appeared empty except for the Grande Dame poised on a simple wooden stool. She held a large, ancient-looking book with an ornately carved leather binding spread open on her lap—white gloves on her hands to protect this priceless, historic volume from any harm due to skin oils and such.

She looked elderly, not in some disparaging way at all. Maybe the better word to describe her would be 'grandmotherly'—not tall, a bit full-figured, and finely dressed in a rich black gown with white trimmings. Her silvery hair tied up into a neat bun, highlighted by rich pink bougainvillea flowers woven here and there framing her rounded and friendly face—endowed with bright eyes and an endearing smile brightening the room.

People have tried to find the right words to describe her. "Special." "One of a kind." "Courageous." "Compassionate." The best adjective capturing her, I think, is "whole." "She is who she is"— one of the best things to be said about any person.

If you knew her whole story, you would agree she is a miracle—very special. Her dark skin marked by wrinkles and crow's feet, and yes, even scars—bore evidence of a compelling life jam-packed with great stories of her own. I assure you, with more time, each of her adventures would be well worth hearing. But, of course, that will have to be another story for another day.

The Royal Storyteller, Berenice, has arrived. The 'she is who she is' captured the complete attention of this large, expectant audience made up of all the people in the Kingdom, and of course, you as well, to tell the Tale of the Unlikely Prince.

She began.

Not so long ago, in a beautiful kingdom not so very far away, lived a glorious King and his troubled, all-too-human son, Yeled. The story is mostly about Yeled, but the tale definitely cannot be told without this king.

Where should we begin? Well, it begins and ends as it should, with the great King.

The King was a very good King, but, like all kings, often misunderstood and sometimes feared by the people. Yet, no King ever loved or provided more for his people. No one was more loved by the great King than his adopted son, Prince Yeled. And yet, Yeled, well, let's not jump ahead of the story. First things first.

Yeled was only a boy when he was adopted by the King. The legend is—and we all know legends have some truth—the prince's birth parents were killed in a failed coup. Rebels had conspired to overthrow the great King. I am telling you the truth. I wouldn't kid about something so horrific. It had been completely unsuccessful—a foolish matter altogether.

Truth be told, this wise King and powerful warrior could never be overthrown by a mere coup of arrogant usurpers. If you want my opinion, I believe there will be no successful coup—ever.

Since you appear to be interested, let me tell you the actual historical account of events told to me by someone in good authority. The truth is almost always more interesting and bizarre than the Cliff Note versions.

The city managers of Garden City (who will forever remain nameless) rebelled against the good King and his rule. Back then, I am told, Garden City was spectacular, lush and green. It lacked for nothing. Today, if you could visit the barren Garden City and her ruined central park—tragically desolate—why would you?

Oh, let's not forget! A shriveled, disappointing tree in the middle of the old, dusty garden remains—another story all on its own. The only other vegetation to speak of are dusty fig bushes lining the outside of the city walls. The word is they are quite void of any fruit. I suppose you could say they serve very little purpose.

I digress.

The coup took place long before there was any wall around Garden City. It didn't need one back then. All were at peace and lacked for nothing. All the people enjoyed intimate fellowship with the King and felt worthy and loved—in a word—enviable, far beyond what they could possibly earn or deserve. This King, the good King, made it so each would feel honored.

One of our court psychiatrists once said, "Everyone needs someone who is irrationally crazy about them." In this kingdom, that someone was the great King. I am not the only one who thinks so.

As strange as it may sound to modern ears, this King didn't demand the glory or hog all sense of well-being. He could have. But he had a way of spreading it all around, from the young to the old, the well to the infirmed, the tall and short, girl or boy, the educated and non.

One historian of some note recorded these words before the unfortunate uprising. "The people in Garden City experienced honor from the King just like everyone else. They knew no shame, only worth. They didn't need to wear a stitch of clothes as they did their daily routines around the garden."

I can't imagine—but it's a fact. They just weren't concerned with how they looked to other people. No one worried if they were or weren't people of value or whether they were attractive to others. I'll freely admit this sounds like I made it up—but I promise, this was the way it was. I have checked the facts closely.

So, it surprised everyone when it happened. The great rebellion, I mean. No one, including my source, can answer the "why?" question. Why did the two city managers start a tragic, silly, stupid and horrible rebellion against the great King's rule?

Yet the rebellion went on for years.

At one point, the city managers' birth son, Yeled...Oops, did I mention the city managers were husband and wife? Oh, and did I mention Yeled's birth parents were the rebel leaders, long before the

King adopted him? Don't worry; I will clear up any confusion as we proceed.

Where was I? Oh, yes. Yeled, a mere 15 summers old, was chosen to mount a cavalry charge right into the heavily fortified center of the King's siege forces—a horrible idea!

If you had a list of the worst cavalry charges of all time, which would have to include Napoleon at Waterloo, the British charge of the Light Brigade, and the Orcs at the siege of Gondor, this Garden City fiasco would still be at the top—epically bad.

Questions still abound. Did they just have bad intelligence? Did young Yeled impulsively act on his own? Did he do it to earn honor or to prove himself a man? It is hard to say. Me? I suspect he did it to make his father proud of him. Boys do such things. Girls too, I suppose.

Why do I come to this conclusion? I am told on good authority, unfortunately, the last thing his dad passive-aggressively said to Yeled before he launched the charge was "Boy, make your mother and me proud <u>this time</u>."

"This time...???" Are you kidding me? No good father would utter such words to an insecure teenager, would they? If this is true, it explains so much. No wonder he was an unlikely prince—do you know what I mean?

I digress... again.

Military experts agree Yeled's forces didn't have a chance. Virtually all were lost, including Yeled's parents.

Yeled was captured alive, though wounded and very ashamed. To this day, he still carries the noticeable scar from a saber's slash along his left jawline, from the corner of his mouth to just beneath his sideburns. And you know not all scars are external. He just knew he had disappointed his father so much.

The war-weary "freedom lovers" (as they referred to themselves, ironically) in Garden City immediately initiated negotiations for Yeled's safe return.

[Storyteller's note: Some more fashion-forward residents of Garden City even had t-shirts made that said "Got Eleutheromania?" Eleutheromania refers to the intense and irresistible desire for freedom. Freedom from the good King's rule, I suppose. I believe that it is actually eleutherophobia, a fear of freedom. I will leave it for you to decide.]

Back to my story. Multiple high-level envoys were going from gate to gate—the first shuttle diplomacy. Proposals and counterproposals, yet no agreement was found. Not even close.

Why? Because the King demanded justice. And of course, everybody knows the penalty—the only just penalty for such rebellion—was death. There is no exception to the law of the King.

Well, now things have become very interesting. All seemed lost for Yeled. But then....

Early in the morning, right at sunrise, you won't believe what happened! I still can't believe it. You will have to wait just a little.

Harvey knew the last paragraph was a shameless tease, but it worked!

"OK, you've got my interest," he said aloud to no one in particular. "Challenge on! Dr. McClelland. I think I have time for one more chapter. They are quite short after all. Hmmm, chapter two, Sarshalom's Choice. The plot thickens."

Harvey found himself smiling for the first time in a long, long while.

4

SARSHALOM'S CHOICE

"A children's story that can only be enjoyed by children isn't a good children's story in the slightest." C.S. Lewis

The storyteller continued:

So where was I? Oh yes. The early morning was frigid, February, I think. The skies were still dark and overcast. No moon in the sky for a couple of days and quiet—too quiet.

Then, something strange transpired right in front of the heavily fortified Garden City gate. The guards noticed a single figure approaching under a white flag. Another envoy? A messenger? No one was expected. So, who might this be? As the solitary figure drew close, someone recognized him, the King's first-born son, Sarshalom.

Sarshalom was anything but an 'unlikely' prince. Oh no! He was a great prince, tall, brave and a tested warrior. And like his father, he deeply cared for his people. Everyone loved him—well, except for the people of Garden City, I suppose.

I am not a psychiatrist, so I can't begin to explain what happened next. Maybe the townspeople were so tired and frustrated by the long siege. Maybe they were filled with pent-up rage. Whatever. What happened next was not reasonable. The subsequent scene could only be described as subhuman—in a word, shameful.

As soon as the King's son entered Garden City under a banner of peace, the rebels erupted into an ugly mob. They knocked him to the ground with sticks and rocks and brutally beat him. They brought him before a judge, declared him guilty of war crimes and killed him. The whole horrible thing only took a couple of hours. No one had seen anything like it before or since.

In only a few hours, the great prince, the beloved son of the great king, the sole heir to the whole kingdom—including the Garden City—was no more.

Then, if you think it couldn't get worse—it did! The people of Garden City gathered in the rotted garden in the middle of the city and partied until they could party no more. Can you believe it?

You probably want to know what Sarshalom was thinking. Was this a good idea? Was this his way of honoring his father, the king? Or was this just what great princes do to try to make peace, even at great personal sacrifice?

Other people smarter than me believe the prince didn't act on his own. Maybe the strange plan was birthed out of the great King's war room, in cahoots between the King, Prince Sarshalom and the Royal Steward, of course informed by the counsel of the Royal Vizier, Nomos. One has to wonder if this was the only possible way to finally end hostilities and usher in lasting peace and real glory for both sides. I will leave it for you to decide.

Truth be told, hostilities continue unabated to this very day. So much for lasting peace. But did Sarshalom's death bring any real glory? Well, an excellent question and the very heart and soul of our tale, as you will see.

I truly hope Sarshalom's tragic fate hasn't caused you distress. I had to tell you about Sarshalom because it is part of Yeled's story. You will see why in just a little bit.

Let's quickly move on, shall we?

When the report of Sarshalom's tragic death got to the King, he mourned deeply. You probably know great kings mourn greatly. It's a great king thing. His entire kingdom mourned for forty days. At the end of the time of mourning, the King did something so unlikely (I chose this word carefully. Can you guess why?) and yet so magnanimous, it reverberates throughout the land even today. You may be surprised.

The great King formally adopted Yeled—of all people—the erstwhile offspring of the deceased rebellious city managers—to be his only son and unchallenged heir to the entire Kingdom. What?

I know what you are thinking—I am making this up, right? But would I kid about something so mystifying and at the same time, so resplendent? I'm telling you; this is exactly what happened. Unbelievable, but, hey, there it is.

I've spent a lot of time pondering the whole tragic Sarshalom event. Here's the only way I can explain it. While the rebels did the one thing they thought would shame the great King the most, the great King did the one thing he hoped would bring the most honor to the most people of Garden City.

What honor? You ask a lot of great questions. From now until eternity, the bloodlines of the great King and the people of Garden

City are forever intertwined. Are you with me? Fascinating, am I right?

Whew, time to take a breath and regroup. I have covered so much, so quickly. Let me step back and give a summary. I don't want to lose anyone. This is too great a story.

Ready? Yeled, the first-born son of the rebellious city managers, is now the adopted son of the great King. He is the sole heir of all the Kingdom. An 'unlikely' prince, to be sure—and so the book's title. Are we good?

What might Yeled be thinking? Let's have some fun. Let's do an interactive survey. You tell me what you think. Just raise your hand. Which of the following statements do you think most reflect what Yeled is thinking as the newly adopted yet unlikely prince?

1. *I can't believe my good fortune.*

2. *I feel so loved now by my new father, the King.*

3. *I really need to make my new father proud of me. I can't be a disappointment to him like I was with my birth father.*

Hmmm, very interesting. Thanks for participating. Just looking out over the audience, while I can't exactly count all the votes, clearly, most of you think #1, "I can't believe my good fortune."

We will see. But to mention the obvious, we are just at the beginning of my tale of honor, quests and fellowship. Legends are made of such, and the Tale of the Unlikely Prince is an extraordinary legend if I humbly say so myself.

At Prince Yeled's coronation, all came, all bowed low (because bending the knee is what you do, even if you are not totally on board). All did homage to the new royal.

They did so, not because Yeled had done anything to earn it. In fact, the only thing on his resume was the unfortunate cavalry charge which is still studied to this day in the kingdom's military school as an example of how not to do a charge.

No, in this kingdom, Prince Yeled's new glory was solely due to the glory of his adoptive father, the great king.

It certainly wasn't based on the name and reputation of his birth parents. That and $5.00 will get you a latte from the castle's barista (tip not included). By the way, my favorite is the double mocha butter candy latte with a little whipped cream. Try it.

I digress again. Thank you for your patience. So much to say in such little time. Back to our unmistakably superb tale.

The people bowed to the new prince because the King proclaimed Yeled's new adoption—some would say 'ascribed' glory. I have come to refer to it as 'so be'd' worth or status. The King proclaimed, "So be it!" And it was. The unlikely prince is now the so-be'd prince. I'll say more.

The final words of the Great King reverberated through the Great Hall and surprised so many, and at the same time, moved many to tears.

"This is my beloved Son, with whom I am well pleased."

...and so Yeled was officially so-be'd!

The Royal Sociologist says this practice is common in honor and shame cultures. In most other cultures, your reputation and worthiness are largely based on what you accomplish—what you earn, so to speak. She calls it 'achieved' glory. It is self-explanatory.

If this tale happened in a different place, Prince Yeled would likely be in a probationary period no doubt for a long time. Former rebels would need to prove themselves worthy of any honor. I could tell such a story too, I suppose, but it would not be anywhere near as breathtaking as this one.

In cultures such as ours, glory is mostly so be'd by someone of greater glory. Here, the only way to get glory and remove the lingering shame of past mistakes is for the king to share his or her glory with you. The king singlehandedly, for purposes known only to himself, transforms the shamed one into an honored one. Simple, right?

There. Clear for everyone? If this so-be'd concept is new to you, no worries—you will pick it up as we proceed.

So, the formerly shamed Yeled immediately became a person of great glory because the Great King said, "So be it."

For those of you who are paying attention, this does not mean the unlikely prince feels glorious. In fact, for you English majors, who are trying hard to identify the main narrative conflict driving our tale, you need wonder no more.

Yeled is the prince but doesn't feel much like a prince—or at least a worthy prince. In fact, he feels just the opposite. He thinks everyone sees him as a disappointment. It seems his birth father just never got around to telling him how special he was. It seems many young princes and princesses aren't very sure if their fathers—and mothers—are proud of them. It is very sad.

You may be thinking I am being way too hard on Yeled's father. I thought so too when I first heard the story. But the Royal Psychiatrist assures me it doesn't really matter whether his father was a 9 or a 2 on the "good enough parent spectrum." What matters is what Yeled heard. I have come to agree.

Yeled thought about it a lot and constantly worried. "Do all who proclaim me 'prince,' in fact, resent my title?"

He imagined them making jokes behind his back, just expecting him to fall on his face. Why? Like the rest of us, he had a nasty little critical dragonesque voice inside him that never missed an opportunity to remind him of his checkered history.

"Well, you were the son of the anti-King rebels. Oh, and you were the failed commander of the worst military charge of all time. Oh, and did I mention your adoption cost the life of the very popular Prince Sarshalom, the true firstborn of the Great King?"

But at the top of his self-condemnation list? "You have already failed one father. You will likely disappoint your new dad too."

And so, the title of our tale. Yeled is the 'unlikely' prince.

So, what can he do? In his mind, he must do something grand, something stunning, something truly praiseworthy. What would it be? He will ask the king for a quest—no, a great quest. Oh, this is getting exciting. Are you feeling it too? I wonder if it will work.

Harvey quickly checked his watch to see how late it was getting. Not too bad he determined. He truly felt for the young man, their shared sense of loss and struggle creating a bond. "He's had a tough go, for sure. Neither of us had an old man who told us they cared. But what about his new father, the Great King?"

His curiosity was piqued, and he turned the page with eager anticipation to the next chapter.

5

THE MAKING OF A GREAT COAT OF ARMS

T he storyteller continued her tale.

My inside sources, who claim to be in the know, informed me the King had his greatest craftsmen design a unique glorious coat of arms suitable for a glorious prince.

Reportedly, it took the better part of a month for the right design to be presented to the King. The King was ecstatic with the results. He ordered Prince Yeled to receive no blanket, towel, shorts or robe not embroidered with the new coat of arms. The order covered all cups, plates, saddles and even toothbrushes.

Everyone knows there can be no prince and no real quest without an appropriate coat of arms. And no great prince is without a great coat of arms. It is the rule of quest storytelling.

This prince had an unequaled coat of arms. Truly, in all the land, before or since, there has not been a more effulgent coat of arms.

[Storyteller's Note: Just making sure we check all the right boxes. All great quest stories must use the word 'effulgent' at least once.]

The coat of arms contained a tri-part royal blue shield beneath a regal rampant lion with a red tongue and fierce claws. The lion stood atop and engaged in crushing a lion-headed dragon beneath his massive paws.

In the upper left third of the shield read the ancient word "mishpat" on top of judicial scales. In the upper right the similarly ancient word "tzedakah" lay inscribed on top of a red heart. In the bottom third section the phrase "lipnay melek" above a mother gazing into the eyes of her infant completed the unrivaled coat of arms—so exquisite!

What did the strange words mean? Well, I will tell you, just be patient.

As I said, there can be no good quest story without a prince and his coat of arms consisting of mysterious, strange words constructing a bit of a riddle. No good quest story begins with the prince already understanding what his coat of arms means. Fun, right?

But what in the world do those words mean? I will tell you, but you could have just as easily googled it. Mishpat is an ancient Hebrew word referring to 'justice.' It's a little different than what we mean by justice today.

Let me see, how can I explain mishpat? Think of a time when someone hurt you, treated you poorly, or took something from you. All you wanted was for things to be made whole again. The hurt gone. What was taken brought back to you. Mishpat is about making a wronged person right again.

Tzedakah (pronounced tsĕ-dah-kah) is similar and different too. They are often used together. It literally means right but is better understood relationally—to be right with someone else. You get it, right?

[Sorry, my bad]

If you are right with someone else, you are going to treat them right. So, the tzedakah person might see someone who is sick or hurting. They want the person to get well again. They see hunger and want to provide food. They see slaves, and they want them to be free.

Both are great qualities for a prince or princess—am I right? The tzedakah thinks of others first, even if it costs them greatly. Remember Sarshalom? There has never been a more 'mishpat' or 'tzedakah' royal, ever, and maybe never will be again. He so wanted to make unfair things in the kingdom fair again and to take care of the hurting people, even those in Garden City.

Lastly, the strange ancient Hebrew phrase 'lipnay melek' is by far the hardest to understand, I think. It is very important. I will give you a clue. It literally means 'in front of the King's nose.' Hmm, not very helpful, I suppose. Well, over the years, it picked up the sense of being 'in the presence of the King,' –still a bit confusing and unclear. No worries. Its meaning will be unpacked later, you have my word as the royal storyteller.

Yeled will struggle to figure this one out, and it is the heart of the quest. Maybe we can help him? Don't worry; the quest will unlock all the mysteries.

While I personally love the turn of a good ancient phrase, all storytellers know the importance of clarity. The Unlikely Prince is a story for young adults, after all. So instead of repeating 'mishpat,' 'tzedakah,' and 'lipnay melek,' let me simplify them. Great princes and princesses should 'make things whole,' 'do right for others' and 'never leave the King's presence.' Good rules to live by, to be sure.

Is everyone still on board? Good.

How will the audience know when Yeled finally gets it? Such a silly question. In his quest, the prince will not become smarter, taller, stronger or more handsome. He will not become a better cavalry officer. No, not at all. The quest is successful once the prince not only comes to see the meaning of his coat of arms but, more importantly, is changed in light of the three mysterious riddles. In a real sense, he "becomes" the prince. But he is far from there right now at the beginning of our tale.

Why am I telling you? Well, I am guessing you have been down a few quests. Everybody knows failed quests have consequences.

So far, this has only been an explanatory introduction. Are you ready to get into the quest? Let's go!

This time, Harvey didn't even stop to check his watch. Immersed in what he was doing, he wasn't even thinking—his brain on autopilot.

Some people are that way when they run, carve wood, or paint. Harvey was never in that mode, until tonight. He was caught up in the pages of the *Unlikely Prince* and about to embark on his own quest.

Before he turned the page, his last stray thought was, "El must never know that I was reading her children's book."

6

THE PRINCE'S PROBLEM

T he storyteller went on:

So, we spoke about the prince's history and the all-important coat of arms. We also did some very important character development of Yeled—critical for a good story. We used the word 'effulgent' already, and we are only in chapter four. Could it get any better? Oh, yes. We also learned a few mysterious ancient words. Very cool. I think we are ready to get into the actual quest. I can't wait.

We catch up with the prince having an official audience with his father, the great King.

"Father," said the tall, wiry young man. He was not a day over eighteen now, with a head full of long dark hair tied back, emphasizing his broad jaw and—shall we say, more-than-forthright nose. The prince said it very confidently and appropriately, speaking with such a king. He had practiced this speech for some time. It was obvious.

Yet, I will tell you, just beneath his protective surface, he was very anxious. This was a huge moment for Yeled. If the King refused his request, he didn't know what he would do. He couldn't prove it, but he was still sure others in the court made fun of him behind his back.

He imagined them saying, "Look at him! The usurper boy-prince is the son of rebels. Who does he think he is? We know the truth. He is just an empty showpiece of the King's magnanimous grace, nothing more. Why, he couldn't even make his real father proud of him. Sure, he is so-be'd, but he's a disgrace."

Were these real voices or just the paranoid utterings of the unlikely prince's critical inner voice? No judgment. We all have such a nasty dragon inside our brain, a little or a lot. What makes it worse? It sounds like our own voice—or our mothers and fathers. Either way, the voices were painfully real to him. That's the point, isn't it?

"Father," said the prince with an exaggerated conviction. "I request your permission to begin my quest. I have studied under Royal Vizier Nomos for three years now. I believe I have learned all I need to begin my rightful quest. I won't mess this one up. (He emphasized the word 'this.') I want to finally earn the right to be the prince at last."

Nomos was not only the highly respected Royal Vizier, but he was also the prince's trusted trainer. Since he was so-be'd, Yeled could not remember a day without Nomos. Nomos was a short, burly man with an unruly shock of very white hair. He was a bit portly, reminding Yeled of a large garden gnome. His boyish blue eyes lit up when he cracked a joke. But he could also be quite impatient with students. No one treated him lightly, that's for sure.

I would be remiss not to tell you this about Nomos. He was very Scottish if you know what I mean. He usually wore a thick cotton shift. With each step he took his stiff leather sandals would loudly snap, foreshadowing his presence. On more formal occasions, he would wear a very colorful tartan kilt. Kilts are a kind of skirt for men (but don't let Nomos know I told you). He often donned a red cap. Nomos preferred calling it a Kilmarnock bonnet. Also, his very strong accent required Yeled to request a translation of the numerous sayings he dropped on the young man.

He referred to Yeled once as 'Skinny Malinky Longlegs!' – A tall and skinny person.

Once, Yeled came to class inappropriately attired. Nomos blurted out, "Is the cat deid?" Has the cat died? This means your trousers are too short. I kid you not. Who knew?

For a long time, his teacher intimidated Yeled. But after a while, Yeled began to appreciate his quirky and playful ways. But like I said, Yeled understood no one should ever take Nomos lightly. He was not a man to be trifled with. Not at all.

Once, Yeled dropped a Scottish-ism on the master. It took a bit of research, but he was ready and waiting for just the right time. In one class, Nomos repeated a part about how sneaky some dragons can be in the heat of the chase. This was old news. Yeled raised his hand to get acknowledged and said with a smirk,

"Dinna teach yer Granny tae suck eggs!" Meaning stop teaching someone something they already know.

They both laughed so hard the class could not be continued. Yeled felt very fortunate to have such a great mentor.

Nomos began to train Yeled in earnest shortly after his adoption three years before. The prince, only fifteen summers at the time, did everything Nomos asked of him and more. Some might suggest he was driven—as if he desperately needed to clear himself of the dark legacy of his birth parents and, of course, the tragic cavalry charge. The truth is, he wanted to make his new father proud—maybe his old father as well.

In one sense, Yeled had it all. And yet, in another sense, he still felt like he didn't belong. "If only they knew my deepest thoughts and fears, they would toss me out on the streets," he said to the mirror one evening. It was totally not true, but to Yeled, nothing could be more real.

To make matters worse, he was living in the former first son's grand bedroom. Can you imagine? He just didn't feel comfortable there. If only he could do something great to finally gain the King's favor and make a name for himself—wouldn't the King feel differently about him then? Wouldn't the people also feel differently about him? He desperately wanted to prove himself to his adoptive father, but he didn't know how.

Then it came to him. He knew exactly what would put him in his father's good graces forever. He needed a quest. No, he needed a great quest—a quest like no other quest. The greatest quest of all time. Maybe then, just maybe, he could rest in his new skin. Maybe then people would forget the past. Maybe he would.

So, he worked hard to prepare. Great quests require even greater preparation. Nomos taught the prince how to do princely things, not just on the battlefield but also in court. Yeled learned the rules of chivalry, civility, honor, faithfulness, loyalty and humility. He learned to fight with a sword, axe, spear, bow and arrow, to ride, joust and wrestle. Under Nomos' tutelage, the prince grew tall and strong, broad-shouldered and confident in his ability to fight. To all *appearances, the prince looked like a real prince. All could see his grace, his education, his stature and, of course, his hygiene.*

You have probably heard some other princes forsake their monthly baths. Remember, this is real, not just some Disney fantasy.

Princes, no doubt, have their reasons for this unfortunate oversight. It puts the people of the land in a very awkward position, as you can imagine. They definitely notice a prince's hygiene. Who wouldn't? Likewise, who would ever tell a prince to his face he smelled of horse-offing?

In the prince's defense, soaps back then were very caustic and caused red spots in awkward places. No one had thought of adding a quarter of moisturizing cream or manufacturing a floating soap. Such a novelty would seem silly to grizzly soap makers who render pig fat in huge, rusty, old iron vats. Fortunately, this prince was careful to make full use of his allotted monthly baths. He was proud of his hygiene.

Shhhh! Can I tell you another little secret about the prince? He had been suffering from horrible nightmares as of late. In his dreams, the King's first son shows up at the palace and retakes his rightful place as the King's true heir. The King lovingly embraces his first son and announces publicly how proud of him he is. Yeled is disgraced and tossed out on the cold, unfriendly streets. The people surround him and throw rotten fruit and goat dung at him, cursing his name—of course in a cockney accent. All quest tale mobs speak old street English. But you probably already knew that.

"Now look at him, the wannabe royal. Just a fake son, a usurper, a deceiver. What were you thinking, boy? Your so-be'ing was just for show. Unworthy, unworthy, unworthy!"

Yeled shared the dreams with the Royal Steward. She was so wise in these matters. Yeled always felt safe with her—even more than with Nomos.

This is the first time I mentioned her—but it won't be the last. Take note of this amazing woman. She is a very important character in the prince's ultimate quest. In fact, she holds a very important key to understanding the mysterious coat of arms. Remember? Mishpat, tzedakah, and lipnay melek? Good on you. Back to the steward.

The Royal Steward was a thin, mature woman of color—not unattractive, Yeled thought to himself. Her face was adorned with wrinkles due to her age. Her almost white hair was tied behind her neck with a thin blue ribbon. She typically wore a brown, rough-textured, woolen robe. A full hood draped over her steely blue eyes. Her small feet were adorned with simple, open sandals. Her entire persona exuded empathy and humility. Simply put, she cared for people. They felt it in her presence. It was quite a gift.

She spent most of her time with Yeled just listening. I would describe it this way. She didn't prattle like some others in the court. The truth is she rarely spoke, and so each of her words felt weighty somehow. And when she did speak, her voice was of the heavens, dulcet and soothing.

It was said her words and tone could make a troll weep. You probably know trolls are very nasty beasts. The Royal Steward would argue they are just tragically misunderstood creatures. Above my pay grade. But I am not going to test it, believe me.

What did she and the prince talk about? She just kept reminding the prince about the unending and unchanging love of his adopted father, the great King, and how much the great King was already proud of him, quest or no quest.

As Yeled described his nightmares, the Royal Steward replied, "Remember, young prince, such are troubling dreams—but only dreams." Her eyebrows were knit together in compassion, concern or both. "Though it is hard to believe, the King adores you as much as he ever adored His first-born son, Sarshalom. No more, no less. He has no regrets. Sorrows? Sure, but no regrets."

"You can do nothing to earn more of the King's love," she assured the prince once again. It was obvious to observers Prince Yeled wasn't ready to hear it—not yet anyway. Sometimes princes can be stubborn and self-absorbed, and insecure princes even more so.

"You can't lose even a sliver of the King's love for you," she said emphatically. "He is irrationally crazy about you. The King's love never hesitates, never pulls back and never stops loving. The great King doesn't know how to abandon or turn his back. He is so proud of you. You need not—you cannot—earn more of his love. It may feel like you need to do something more. I understand and sympathize with you. Yet, you are the King's son. Dwell on your relationship with him. When you are lipnay melek (there's the mysterious phrase on the coat of arms) in the presence of your father, make sure you look into his eyes. Then you will know."

"If you want to worry about something, worry about the nasty, critical inner voice inside your head clearly not serving you well. A nasty dragon seems to want you to think you are a disappointment. He will greedily gobble up any thoughts about your worth. Please hear me, prince. Look up into your father's eyes, his measuring gaze. Then these dreams will diminish and perhaps pass—yet not without daily effort on your part, I suspect. Shame's roots go deep."

Unfortunately, the dreams didn't pass. In fact, they happened more often. I share these intimate details about the prince with you so *you will understand him better. He is not alone. It turns out many princes—and princesses—can relate. Maybe you?*

Oh my. I am not so sure he is ready for a quest, are you? Don't you need to have it all together when you face a fierce dragon, or two, or a dozen? One misstep, one little hesitancy, one distraction because you didn't get enough sleep due to some recurring nightmare—and BOOM, you're done!

And we were just beginning to like Prince Yeled. Maybe, just maybe something's at play we are not aware of? I hope so.

Back to the prince.

7

DEEPER THOUGHTS

"To begin is the most important part of any quest and by far the most courageous." Plato

"It's definitely time to call it a night," said Harvey. He couldn't remember the last time he had been able to relax like this. It was as if he had been transported to the fictional auditorium or maybe even into that royal throne room. It just made him smile. Busy people like Harvey, particularly business owners, find it tough to take breaks. People depend upon them, and after all, who has the most to lose if the business doesn't make it or doesn't thrive?

Harvey took another gulp of bourbon. It was so good. He liked its caramel smoothness, and it wasn't too sweet like some other off-the-shelf stuff.

"It's funny what you think about when you let your hair down a bit." Harvey's thoughts went to his friend, Ron's, funeral. Family and well-wishers packed the place. He was a very popular and influential man. His eldest son, Joe, gave a fantastic eulogy. In tears, he called his dad a gentle giant. The description fit him perfectly, and an understanding chuckle reverberated through the church's auditorium.

Young Joe had followed his dad's career path, even signing on to Goldman a few years back. Ron was bursting with pride for his son. They would often talk about their jobs and hash out issues. It looked like Joe was on a fast track. Ron would brag about him for at least 18 holes.

At the end of the eulogy, Joe toasted his father and his father's legacy with a tumbler of Glen. Pastor Rick didn't mind. It was a beautiful scene. All over the church, people were in tears. Harvey's eyes got moist, too. He didn't feel comfortable admitting it to El then, but he wasn't heartless. He just quickly wiped them away with his jacket sleeve.

Harvey was genuinely happy for Joe, but if he were to be brutally honest, he couldn't help but feel a twinge of jealousy. No, scratch that. He was furious—not at Ron or Joe, but at himself. He had messed up his family, a couple of families.

He had tried to get his eldest son, Bo, into the business. Bo was extremely bright and had a business degree in finance from a local college. Harvey had given him an internship at his shop, and things appeared to be going great. They were even beginning to chat more—some actual bonding. Their relationship became a friendship, mentorship, and shared passion for business. Harvey couldn't have been happier. He was so proud of his son.

But then, out of the blue, Bo announced he didn't want to work at Harvey's company. He said he wanted to make his own way, his own path, yes, his own quest—so to speak.

Harvey admitted he didn't handle it very well and blew up at his son. That was that.

They still talk some—mostly at holidays and birthdays. Bo and his new wife and family—two great young boys—moved across the country and joined up with an outfit consulting with Fortune 500 companies.

Ultimately, Harvey was proud, but above all, he was sad. What was he going to do with his business? His other son, James, had joined the Navy and never called. It was a good fit for him. He needed the structure.

Harvey took another hit from the glass tumbler and turned to the next page of the book.

It was time for the great quest, which was clearly the night's theme. "Am I on a quest?" Harvey questioned. So much for calling it a night—he was eager to read on. He turned the page. He could almost hear the storyteller's voice.

8

The Official Request

"To new beginnings. To the pursuit of...somethingness."
Cecelia Ahern

The storyteller went on:

As the fairly hygienic prince stood before the great King, he pointed at the coat of arms on his vest.

"My King, I would test my mettle to prove my worth to you under the most challenging circumstances. How else would I ever know? How else would you ever know, Father?

O great King, you deserve such a princely prince who makes you smile when you consider him, whose reputation brings you glory and honor, about whom you would want to brag: 'This is my son; I am well pleased with him.' I want to be such a prince. Honor me with a quest—nay, an unprecedented quest. I must be sure."

"In short," (it should be noted princes are rarely short with their speeches) "I would like to prove myself worthy of your favor. I would hear you say to me in private and in public, 'Well done, my faithful son.' I would prove to everyone in court I am more than just a foster child, a creation of circumstance, an adopted orphan to whom so much has been given but not deserved. I do not want to be the 'unlikely' prince anymore. I want to deserve the title and to show you, the Royal Steward and Nomos I am worthy. I want to know you love me—yea verily—even like me. I promise I will do this in the name and memory of your first-born son."

Yeled paused to catch his breath but realized all were staring, a bit shocked.

"I need to prove my worth to myself as well," he said as he placed his hand over his heart. "I want to see a true prince looking back at me in the mirror. Oh, great King, I beg you. Give me my quest—my great quest. I will do it."

The King stared into the eyes of the young man for what felt like a very long time. There was little emotion on his face—not pleasure, pride, criticism or disappointment—nothing the prince could discern anyway. After a pregnant pause, a royal tear formed in the King's royal eye and ran down his royal face. This King was a very emotional King. His empathy and compassion for all were legendary. The prince's request moved the King. Good or bad? I will leave it for you to speculate.

Finally, the uncomfortable silence ended. The King silently nodded to the prince and began to speak. His words were not just for the prince but for all witnesses throughout the land.

"Let it be known to all," the great King boldly proclaimed as he stood over the kneeling young man. "The prince has requested and will be given a substantial quest—nay, a great quest due a great *prince. Yea verily. He will receive a quest worthy of a great king. At the end of said quest, this prince will know (the King emphasized the word 'will' so much no one, except perhaps the prince, missed it)—he will at last know his place in my heart."*

The great King's resplendent voice echoed throughout the imposing chamber. The people bowed. A resonating silence followed. It seemed the whole creation paused.

When the prince, who also had bowed his head, opened his eyes, he happened to see the King turn to Nomos and wink.

"Strange," the prince thought to himself. He would have to consider this later.

"Royal Vizier Nomos," the King said directly to Nomos with a smile. "Your work is complete. It would seem your student has learned all he can from you. We trust it has been sufficient for the rigors of a quest. Such a quest will test his mettle, stretch his character and steel his passions."

Nomos bowed to the King. Then he lumbered over to Prince Yeled, stretched up to his very tiptoes and kissed him on both cheeks—a Scottish thing, I suppose. It was an odd sight. Yeled was well over six feet. And Nomos—well, Nomos wasn't even close. "Aye, the air is so much better down 'ere," Nomos joked. No one else thought so.

Nomos whispered something into the prince's ears, just for him to hear. I have it on good authority that he said, "You've got this, my lad. I am already proud of you."

[Storyteller note: Remember how different this was from what his birth father told him before the unfortunate cavalry charge?]

After one more endearing glance, Nomos gave Yeled a broad, toothy grin and exited the great hall, his sandals snapping with each step.

A little secret? Nomos was not surprised at the prince's request. Not in the least. Questing is in the very nature of young princes—and princesses, for that matter. Royals are very human after all and feel they must 'do' in order to 'be'. It was not Nomos' job or his skill mix to disabuse such notions from the minds of insecure young princes or princesses. A quest was in order. You will see what I mean.

"My beloved son," the King said as he looked compassionately at the prince. "All this and every aspect of the quest will be accomplished. There will be no failure. You will find what you are looking for. There will be no veering to the right or left, no hesitancy, no disappointment, for any negligence or dereliction at all would be quite consequential. Is this clear? Be aware, this quest involves something far more dangerous, disturbing and unsettling than you can imagine—or be trained for. More than you know right now. There are worse things than the dragons you will come upon out there. Is this also clear?"

"I hear and obey," said the prince, hardly listening now as he was about to explode with excitement. It's a curse of the young, I suppose. No doubt, he was thinking ahead to the many glories waiting for him. Who could blame him? He was going to earn the favor of a father at last, he hoped.

"Prince," the King continued. "This quest will be accomplished through many trials and great tribulations. Your experience of your core prince-ness is at hand."

"I also decree the Royal Steward will come alongside of you. She will not carry a sword or spear. She will not intervene in your quest. She will not fight dragons. No. Her role is to be my presence, my heart, my eyes, my ears and to offer you truth and encouragement. She will remind you of my love and how proud of you I am already. You will need this at times. I am sure."

This was the moment Yeled had dreamed about for a long time and was the most frightened of as well. Yeled knew his life would never be the same, nor would he ever be seen the same by others.

"It is all up to me now," he thought to himself. "Am I that prince? Can I do princely? Can I earn the right to be in the presence of the King and expect my father's pleasure and favor in return? Can I make a father of mine proud? My whole future is mine to conquer. I am ready. Let my quest begin."

I don't know about you; I have high expectations for this prince. This is a marvelous tale, wouldn't you agree? It is time.

Harvey continued reading.

9

THE GREAT QUEST BEGINS

"Quests always have their ups and downs," rumbled the giant. "The point is never to give up, even if you're falling off a cliff. You never know what might happen on the way to the bottom." Nancy Farmer

The storyteller went on:

The excited prince woke up early the next day and put on his serious battle face—no fanfare or pretense. It was time. He was fitted with a linen undershirt and pants. Woolen stockings covered his legs and draped down to his pointed, closed leather boots. On top of the underclothes was a padded gray doublet to prevent the chainmail from chafing him as he rode his royal stallion and fought his enemies. It could be a long journey to get to where the dragons were.

The chainmail was polished and shiny, quite substantial, covering most of his arms and stretching down below his waist. The body armor was covered by an impressive red and black surcoat emblazoned with the official coat of arms.

On his head, he wore a flexible chainmail coif covering his throat, neck and top part of his shoulders. His sword, one the King had given him, was proudly strapped to his side. The prince was indeed ready. He looked very princely, to be sure.

With some difficulty due to the weight of his armor, he mounted his tall, majestic steed and left the great castle with spirit and his head held high. The crowd cheered.

The King's Royal Steward humbly rode alongside the prince on an old gray donkey, at least as old as she was. They were quite a pair, to be sure.

The prince had worked very hard, more than most princes, to emotionally prepare himself for this moment. He knew what was required of a successful prince—or so he thought. For three years, Nomos taught him the expectations. You remember? Princes are expected to 'make things whole' and 'do the right things for others.' Oh, there was a third item on the coat of arms? Hmmm, what was it? The prince couldn't remember, which was too bad.

More importantly—at least in his head—he knew how to fight, how to ride a horse, how to defeat dragons, gnomes, some emotionally misunderstood trolls and even very large elves. It was not well known, but back then there were some very big and very mean elves. This was no small task.

The prince knew how to travel light. He knew how to set up camp, how to cook on an open fire, how to get fruit stains out of badly soiled carpets and was even quite skilled at origami; some say he was as good as Jeremy Shafer. He didn't expect to need origami, but one never knows.

He definitely missed Nomos more than he imagined he would.

The pair journeyed south toward the rugged hill country where there had been reports of dragons rummaging through sheds at night and even absconding with the odd sheep, pig or bumbleberry pie. The people of the hill country were known for their pies. Dragons are no fools.

But given the choice, dragons would still prefer pigs. It's not just the taste. But hey, who doesn't like bacon? Do you know what's better than bacon? More bacon, of course. I digress.

But there's more to the matter. Sheep's wool can easily get caught between the dragon's back teeth. They don't floss. I will explain in a moment. They hate the feeling of something stuck in between their back molars. I get it.

A couple of days out from the presence of the King, the quest went south, metaphorically. They found a dragon or two or three—in fact, a lot. The region was seething with dragons.

In a period of three days, the prince fought ten dragons. There were a variety of sizes, colors and temperaments. It seemed the practice dragons the prince had fought in the castle were generally smaller, slower and tamer than the ones in the real world. Who knew?

This was going to be harder than he thought. As I prepared to tell this story, I researched dragons a lot. Did you know the name "dragon" comes from the Latin *draconem*, which coincidentally means "dragon?" Not so helpful, am I right? It can also refer to their "deadly glance." It's a bit more interesting, isn't it?

Dragons are universally misunderstood. Most people think they all breathe fire. Actually, very few dragons spew fire. None of the dragons the prince fought did. Fire breathing requires a very high-carbohydrate diet with a great deal of oily fats. Most dragons can't afford such a diet. By far, most of the dragons, at least in this kingdom, didn't breathe fire. They coughed a lot though.

And unfortunately, most of them had very bad breath. Horrible, in fact. It should be of little surprise. Remember the issue with sheep? Dragon arms and fingers cannot support flossing and so food gets stuck between their pointy bicuspids for days or weeks. Yuck!

One such halitosis-affected dragon happened to get very close to the prince's face and breathed out all over him. The horrific smell of the dragon's breath stunned the prince. The effluvia caused the prince to faint. For those who are ill-trained in the English language, 'effluvia' refers to the toxic smell of rancid decaying matter—in a word, "YUCK!" Here's another word: "STINKY!" Or "PEE-YOU!" You get the general idea. It was so bad; the prince had blocked out the event for years. By the time the prince's head cleared, the dragon was long gone. Score one for the dragons.

One very fast and vocal dragon wore a baseball cap backwards on its bulbous green, scaly head. A little-known fact. Dragons were into baseball long before humans. There was an entire dragon baseball league with ten teams, playoffs and sponsors. The Birmingham Yellow Wings were dominant—three championships in five years. Lately though, the London Red Scales have been quite a challenge.

This dragon was apparently a member of the Manchester Funny-Looking Feet. They were at the bottom of the league. One wonders if it has something to do with their name. I will leave it for you to decide.

Why baseball? The dragons attempted soccer. But think about it. Twenty-two dragons running around a grass field—with huge claws—left the pitch shredded and unusable for the next team. And you could always find a huge single dragon to squat in front of the net. Who could score? The usual final score was 0-0. It was not much fun to watch. And don't get me started on the dragon basketball tournament.

Yeled struggled to get his mojo going. He chased one of the slower dragons for a while, but it turned out to be a very large turtle dressed up to look like a dragon. Everyone knows turtles are quite insecure. And let's face it, every reptile wants to be a dragon. They are way cool. The aspiring dragon didn't fool Yeled—well, not for very long anyway. Yeled shook his head and laughed at himself as the turtle-dragon slowly crawled away.

Anyway, where was I?

By the end of the third day, the dejected prince was a pitiful, rumpled sight. He could only slump in front of his campfire, licking his many wounds. He took the time to review the play-by-play of the quest so far.

Three of the smaller dragons had bitten and scarred him up quite badly. He didn't expect them to be so fast and so mean. He also got a nagging, tiny little splinter in his right index finger. Of course, splinters are the worst. Am I right?

Fortunately, the Royal Steward knew first aid. She was an accomplished healer and a bit of an expert in the ancient art of splinter removal. Some can do it well, others...not so much.

Still, Yeled was very disappointed in his efforts so far. He had not turned away from the fight, yet it would hardly be called a victory by any measure. He had the external and internal scars to prove it. He didn't want to dwell on it. Five of the larger, slower dragons got away untouched.

Three-day scorecard: Yeled-1, Dragons-9. Nowhere near legendary, for sure. One of the dragons he had vanquished didn't put up much of a struggle. He suspected it was quite old and didn't have the wherewithal to fight back. In the end, the defeated dragon limped back into his comfortable cave using an old, knobby cane, coughing and wheezing the whole way.

Yeled counted this confrontation as a victory—his only one. Pretty sad, really—and questionable according to most quest rules. But who was going to take away this lone semi-highlight from the beat-up Yeled?

Yeled hadn't expected to fail—to fall so abysmally short. He had dreamed of this day for months. This quest was supposed to be about his glory and distinction. He needed to prove to everyone—and himself—that he deserved to be a prince. Yet, even though he had fought to the best of his ability, it wasn't enough—so many things he could have done better, quicker and smarter.

He shook his head in disgust and thought back to his training. He didn't remember. Maybe Nomos never taught him this one important little fact about dragon fighting. Dragons are slimy creatures; everywhere they walk they leave a greasy trail. Who knew?

Well, you can guess what happened. The prince found out the hard way. His first dragon was a nasty, very ill-tempered, albeit small, yellow beast with a red breast. The prince chased it into a narrow glade, disappearing into some thick bushes. Unbeknownst to Yeled, the trail abruptly turned sharp left. If anyone missed the turn, they would plunge off a massive cliff and drop into a tall waterfall. At the very last minute, the dragon zigged, then zagged and then zigged again—avoiding the cliff and sure death. The prince tried to do the same but stepped upon a large patch of yellowish dragon slime. Not only couldn't he stop, but he also found himself accelerating toward the precipice.

At the last second, he turned and grabbed some willow branches hanging over the falls, stopping his plunge into the churning rocky waters below. It was an impressive athletic move by the prince. Unfortunately, he lost his princely sword in the process. The King had given him the royal sword on his 15th birthday, and he lost it on the very first day of battle. Could it have gone much worse?

It turns out his bravado in the King's court was a bit of an overstatement. He was a pretty good swordsman, yet he found he wasn't as prepared to fight with a spear or club. Everyone knows dragons are notoriously difficult to kill with spears or clubs—not to mention bows and arrows. Their skin is too thick, and their vital organs are too deep.

It had been a very bad three days, to be sure. He wondered to himself how he had failed so quickly and so completely. Certainly, a real prince would have been better prepared and more skilled than a couple of slimy, overgrown lizards. How could he return to the King and regale him with tales of such little success? How would this record make his father proud?

The King's final words kept echoing in his head.

"My son, all this must be accomplished."

[Storyteller's note: The King actually said, 'will be' accomplished—a very different thing, am I right?]

"There must be no failure, no veering to the right or left, no hesitancy and no disappointment. Any negligence or dereliction would be consequential. Is this clear?"

I am no doctor, but I suspect the prince was becoming quite despondent. True, he did not act like a prince of any distinction. He did not feel like one and was riddled with sadness. "The King will be so disappointed in me," Yeled thought to himself.

Some smart individual invented the word 'bleak' just for this situation. The prince was immersed in shame and self-condemnation.

By the way, we all know what shame feels like. When you mess up so often, you begin to think something is wrong with you. You wonder if you are broken somehow. Are you good enough for people to like you or think about you at all? You look in the mirror and wonder if you are strong enough, smart enough, pretty enough, funny enough, likeable enough, thin enough or in Yeled's case, princely enough. 'Not-enoughness' can be a real problem for people like the prince—and you and me, of course. Not-enoughness can make even princes and princesses very sad.

So where was I? Oh yes, of course.

The prince was not in a good space. He did not do princeliness well—not up to his own expectations—and, he thought, not up to the high standards of his King.

"Surely the King will be disappointed, maybe even disgusted with my puny efforts," the prince complained to himself.

"How can I ever look up into the gaze of my father after this total collapse of princeliness? I can't. How can I wear this coat of arms again?"

"Wait," he exclaimed, "the coat of arms, the three things. I've forgotten them. I can still do them—I should do them—and they will make all this mess a success. Let me see...mishpat. I am to be about making others' situations whole again. I am to look for injustices needing to be made right. Hmmm. I'm not sure what justice has to do with slaying dragons.

Maybe the next one. Tzedakah? Restoring others to rightness, setting prisoners free—that sort of thing. Hmmm. Again, just not a dragon-slaying thing, really. Lipnay melek, in the presence of the king. How do I be in two places at the same time? The kingdom is a long way away now. How can I be in the presence of the King out here? What's the point? Maybe these will be made clearer tomorrow."

THE LAST QUEST

He could only shake his head in confusion. The wonderful coat of arms was of little help, really. The prince, once filled with confidence, was now just not sure what to do. The quest had not started well—okay, it was a bust, but maybe tomorrow. He hoped so but wasn't sure.

The next day was even darker and more overcast (apologies for the easy weather metaphor). There was a deep, biting chill in the air (second apology, please forgive me).

This was a very good time for the Royal Steward to speak to Yeled. She drew close to him, pulled back her hood, and looked directly into the beat-up prince's eyes.

"Prince, please hear me," the gentle woman implored. "Look into my eyes. Indeed, you have suffered great losses in these early days. You have also worked very hard. My encouragement is for you to remember the King's love for you. He does not love you because you are worthy of his love. His love doesn't require worthiness; it makes you worthy. He can't love you any more than he did when you left for this quest, and he can't and won't love you any less. Remember looking up into his eyes just before you left? Hold on to that. Events change out here. There are successes and failures—often they look and feel the same. But your relationship with the King is forever. He is proud of you, Prince Yeled. Remember."

Unfortunately, the prince stopped listening right after "Please hear me." No judgment from me. I have been there. Your self-focused brain doesn't allow you to hear from anyone else. You are not being rude; you are being human. All the prince could think about was how poor a prince he had been. He had been bullied by a couple of stupid, overgrown reptiles. No disrespect to all the smart dragons out there. I am just reporting what the prince's wounded brain was saying.

Now everyone could clearly see he was not worthy, not enough to be the King's son. All he could think about was the shame he had brought upon his stepfather's name. He had now failed two fathers in only three years. He wondered if it was some sort of kingdom record.

For this astute audience, you may have noticed the prince thought of the great King as his 'stepfather' for the very first time. While accurate, I suspect other emotions are at play here. What do you think?

The now increasingly depressed prince began to worry whether he could ever go home again. It would be too painful to see the disappointment in his father's measuring gaze. His only hope was to press on while clinging to a feather-thin chance of things changing. But even he didn't believe that would happen.

Maybe—just maybe—he could salvage a little of his reputation of doing princely—a little bit anyway. He had to. The quest had lost all joy for him. He looked back over his shoulder in the direction of the castle. He thought he could barely see it just over the horizon through the narrow valley. It seemed so far away now.

He could only walk further away from the lipnay melek; the prince's head hung low; his steps heavy. The Royal Steward knew there was nothing she could say—not yet.

Surely, it couldn't get worse. But then....

10

Harvey's Quest

"Do not lose heart, even if you must wait a bit before finding the right thing. Be prepared for disappointment also, but do not abandon the quest." Albert Schweitzer

Harvey awoke with a start, frozen cold in the same place on the same sofa with the same painful neck crick. He had dozed off after the prince's horrific showing with the dragons. But he slept like a baby for the first time in days.

He felt his face and chuckled. He was still wearing his wife's poofy reading glasses. The thought of her reaction, had she been there, made him smile. She would undoubtedly tease him and tell all her coffee-clutch friends how silly he looked, wearing her glasses and reading a kid's book.

It was 5:00 am, and his internal alarm clock was faithful as always. By 5:30, he was out the door with a burned bagel and berry-flavored cream cheese and at the plant by 6:00.

"Let the quest begin," he said in an old English sarcastic voice with a slight note of tragedy. There is no great princely quest on his agenda today. Nope—no glory today. What might the opposite be? To carry the guilt of messing this one up this time—again? Loneliness at the helm of a sinking ship? The distinction of losing it all and laying off even more faithful employees? The loss of all his capital and assets amassed over a fifty-year career—gone?

He had begun his life wanting to be a great prince, eager to complete a great quest and, in the end, earn a reputation filled with some notable distinction and honor. (Not too much, of course. There is a place for princely humility.) He longed for a community who liked him as he was—who didn't feel the compulsive need to change him—where he didn't have to put on his employer mask or fake it when he was hurting, to have a reasonable number of friends, kind of like his golfing crew, where he could laugh out loud, even laugh at himself and his foibles.

He also wanted to go into his retirement financially secure. He didn't want to burden his wife or any other members of his family—he didn't want to live off Social Security. Maybe he would travel—maybe head down to Cancun and golf three months of the year. His wife would laugh at the thought. For decades, he had worked 12-hour days, 6½ days a week (sometimes 7). She said he wouldn't know how to stop. She might be right. It doesn't matter; all of that was up for grabs now.

Harvey's dad had failed to finish his course, and Harvey wouldn't make the same mistake. He would end the family curse once and for all. His company bore his name–that should mean something. It should. It was a legacy of sorts. "Wasn't it?" Harvey asked no one at all.

But not unlike the prince in the tale, Harvey was on the precipice of failing his quest, or so it appeared. Miserably. How disappointed would his dad be now if he were here?

He entered his office, shutting his door with intentionality and sat down behind his dark oak desk. His back was hurting. He didn't need a doctor. He was worried about what to do next, but he had no muscle group to stop his anxiety. "Bad design," he thought. Did he have one more magic trick? He didn't think so. What might Nomos think of him now?

The rest of Harvey's morning was a fitful blur of disappointing meetings, a growing cacophony of excuses, accusations, and other miscellaneous CYAs, not to mention far too many stressful calls with customers and creditors. Harvey had people to do all of that, but at this moment, he only truly trusted himself with the mess.

His number one priority was to figure out how he could convince his banker that increasing his line of credit was a win-win for everyone. In better times, such a request was a slam dunk. However, the uncertainties of the last quarter's numbers didn't make for a compelling financial case this time.

He had one card to play. He didn't want to, but he would have to meet with his old friend and golf partner, Jim, tomorrow morning. After all, Jim had been Harvey's private banker for over a decade. There's history, right? Trust.

Today's task for Harvey was to gather, let's say, "favorable and optimistic" end-of-the-year projections. There were no two ways about it. Without any good news on the income or expense side of the income statement, Harvey and his company would need more than magic. His legacy was looking shaky—his quest—a joke. He was not sure how to break the news to El. That would have to wait. Could he have seen this coming? Could he have handled it differently? Did he delegate too much too soon?

"Can't go there now. Too much to do now to spend much time with a postmortem." Harvey shook his head slowly as he made one more pass-through updated sales projections. He cringed, his back cramping.

Harvey's entire body jerked when his phone rang. He was so focused on reports he had disappeared into the numbers. I am sure you can relate. We have all done it.

It was his secretary, Cheryl. "Harv, there is a messenger package here from Mr. Scooter. Do you want it now?"

Scooter was another friend of Harvey's, not to mention his bi-weekly business coach and the president of his Rotary chapter this year. Scooter had retired five years ago after a very successful hi-tech venture. He was only 50 but sold his business to Google for $2 million.

"Strange," thought Harvey. "We weren't supposed to get together until next week. I may have to reschedule anyway—there's too much going on."

"Sure, bring it in."

Cheryl entered Harvey's office and placed the small package on the paper-covered desk. "This note came with it."

"Hey Harv! Scooter here. Look, I know we aren't supposed to get together this week. Sadie called me this morning and told me what's going down at your place—serious stress. I think I understand. I also know you well enough to predict you will be trying to think of a way to reschedule our meeting next week. Don't. Look, this will sound crazy, my old friend, but I was hoping you could come to my house tonight. I have a special guest you may find fascinating—if not wildly helpful—your call. I am sending you a book by this guy so you can read ahead. I know you don't have much flex in your schedule...so even if you can't read much, still come tonight, 6:30. Just come."

"Oh, and before you ask, I already know it's a kid's book. Don't read too much into that. I must confess; I saw my wife reading it and took it when she wasn't looking. It blew me away. I got a bunch of copies to hand out to friends. Hope to see you tonight. How's El's sister doing? Scooter."

Harvey slowly opened the small package and was beyond shocked. He held a hot-off-the-press copy of "*Tale of the Unlikely Prince*" in his hands. "What in the world was happening here?"

"Do you want me to get back to Mr. Scooter?" Cheryl said in a professional tone.

"No," Harvey replied with a chuckle, surprising his secretary. It had been a while since Harvey had smiled, much less laughed. "Look, I am headed out for some lunch. I will be back in half an hour—or so."

Harvey felt some guilt leaving the sinking ship even for thirty minutes to get a bite to eat and another cup of coffee, but this was too bizarre. First, Eleanor, now Scooter? Was this a conspiracy—or worse—an intervention? Not like Eleanor at all. Coincidence? Also, not likely. And how did Scooter know he was going to reschedule? Was he so predictable?

He ordered a coffee and Reuben from the sandwich shop downstairs. It was his regular, for the few occasions he took time for lunch. This time, the food was mere context. He needed time to think. He needed air. "What's this book all about?" Harvey wondered to himself quietly as he examined the cover again. Was it more than a book for teenagers? Scooter seemed to think so, and the author was at his house tonight. What was the possibility? Was this…could this be a God-thing, whatever that is?"

He had lots of questions and zero answers. "If this was a God thing," he wondered, "God sure is holding His cards close to his heavenly vest. God had never shown much interest in me before. Why now? Not likely," he concluded.

Harvey found a seat in the corner and turned to the place in the *Unlikely Prince* where he had fallen asleep the previous night. "I have time to look at one more chapter. What could it hurt? They are short. Maybe I'll see what Scooter was thinking. Let's see…Hmmm," Harvey said, his right eye arched a bit. "Here it is. I remember a bad first day for the prince. Can it get any worse? Yeah, he could have *my* life!" Harvey relaxed, took a gulp of his dark roast, and smiled. He felt like a kid again.

11

Can It Get Any Worse?

"I don't know anything my parents could have done or left undone which would have saved me from the pincers, mandibles, and eyes of those many-legged abominations" C.S. Lewis

The storyteller went on:

But then it got much worse.

It was getting dark, and so the prince and the Royal Steward pitched their tents in a beautiful, lush glen wedged in between two gently rising slopes. Tall, broad-limbed trees—sycamores, I think—but they could have been large ancient oaks, adorned each rise. I was never good in my botany and dendrology classes. I did pass, though—but just barely.

But enough about me.

There was a bubbling brook filled with cool, clean water running through the middle of the valley. It was a perfect place to settle in and regroup.

How was the prince doing? Not well—not well at all. All the old feelings of failure and disappointment had bubbled up again. It wasn't pretty, but it was very human. This story might just end badly if something doesn't change.

To top it off, there was a lone sign at the edge of the glen—it looked like a warning sign. It read,

"Warning: Beware of the S_____."

The bottom row of the sign had been torn off, making its message incomplete and quite unhelpful.

"Beware of what?" The prince barked at no one in particular. He grabbed the sign off the tree and just shook it, taking out his frustration on it. "Snakes? What does the 'S' mean? Snails? See-Saws? Salad? Salamanders? Are you kidding me? Socks, maybe? Sachets? Sack lunches (well, technically two words—my bad)? Sailboats? Sabre-tooth tigers? Someone's playing a joke on me, right?"

He did add the last one as a joke. Everyone knows sabretooths haven't been seen here for a decade or more.

Then, to make his point, he threw the broken sign onto the ground and stomped on it until it was broken even further. The Royal Steward knew the prince needed to take a step back and breathe, but he wasn't listening. At this point, he couldn't.

This could be a problem. Those of you familiar with epic quest tales like this one probably know Rule #5 of great quests is to never ignore a warning sign—even a confusing one. Anything could happen.

But the prince had forgotten Rule #5 or planned to ignore it out of spite. Instead, the prince decided he had finally earned a moment to relax. He took off the surcoat with the coat of arms stitched to the breast, then his boots and all the chainmail. It felt good. He had forgotten just how heavy it all was. Now he was down to just his linen tunic and pants and the smelly wool socks as a slight chill entered the early evening air. He leaned back and took a deep breath. It didn't seem to help much.

After a few minutes, his training kicked in and he dutifully got up to gather wood. They would need a large warming fire tonight.

In a short time, he and the Steward were comfortably sitting on logs pulled up near the raging blaze; their palms extended to claim all the warmth they could. Getting the fire together distracted him for a time, but now his mind returned to the mess he made of his day.

"I need to take inventory," he thought to himself. "Real knights take inventory of weaponry." In this case, his armory was quite depleted. If anything happened in the darkness of the night, he couldn't rely on his sword. He had lost it on the first day, remember? But he still had his bow and arrow ready at his side. He could shoot—not as good as he could fight with a sword—but he was more than tolerable. He drew out his bow and got an arrow notched in place, just in case.

Little did he know what was about to happen. Well, you can probably guess, can't you?

Completely exhausted, the prince and the Steward quickly fell asleep by the dwindling fire. In fact, the fire didn't make it halfway through the night. With no light from the fire, the campsite was pitch black. Nights are often pretty dark, of course. The moon may be out, and maybe even stars here and there. But then there are nights like this one where there is no moon and no stars. This was more than dark; this was dark, dark, maybe even darkest dark. You get the idea.

In the bowels of this blinding blackness, the prince and the Steward were abruptly awakened by a fierce, high-pitched screeching, maybe a quarter of a kilometer away. It sounded like a crying baby. No, multiple crying babies—dozens, maybe hundreds of them. Neither the prince nor the Steward could see anything beyond a few feet. But what they heard chilled them to the bone. It sounded like a tumult of dark squealing or caterwauling rolling down the valley, coming closer at breakneck speed. It seemed like a wave of sorts but not a flood of water, which has a very distinctly floody sound. It was a roar of pitter-patter, Pitter-Patter, PITTER PATTER—growing in intensity and force—rushing down the glen toward them. Seemingly unstoppable, unhindered and unseen.

The prince realized too late they were in the way of a stampede of some kind—but of what kind? The prince was still half asleep and was now also in shock. He shook his head to remove the cobwebs, and as a precaution, he put an arrow in his bow. He was as ready as he could be. But ready for what?

Well, listeners, it wasn't water or babies. It was spiders—an onslaught of them—that's right, can you believe it? There must have been a million of them, maybe billions of frantic, out-of-control, ugly arachnids. Arachnida (/e'raeknide/) is a class of joint-legged arthropods in the subphylum Chelicerata. Arachnida includes, among others, spiders, scorpions, ticks, mites and vinegarroons—probably more than you wanted to know.

This can't be emphasized enough. The prince really hated spiders! If he were to personally rank the most frightening animals, it would include bees, snakes and bats, but at the very top of the list would be spiders—any spider—even vinegarroons. He automatically shuddered in revulsion. His pulse immediately shot up as his frightened midbrain ignited his fear cycle—cortisol shut down his frontal cortex, the part of his brain where reason dwelt. His mouth dried up and he subconsciously froze in place. He couldn't move, and he couldn't breathe either.

The prince and the Steward were caught in a spider stampede. I did some more research; it had been years since the last spider stampede—long before this prince had been born. No one knows what sets them off, but once unleashed, they can destroy miles of farmland and forests. No one knows how to stop them either. They eventually calm down and go about their daily arachnid business—whatever their daily arachnid business may look like. I did not do well in my entomology class either.

But I digress again.

This was a spider stampede like none other in anyone's memory. There were spiders of all sizes, shapes and dispositions. There were fuzzy ones, striped ones, male and female ones (I suppose they had sexes?), loud ones and quiet ones, tall and short ones. There are more than 45,000 known species of spiders, and they were all headed for the prince.

It was something. The huge brown spiders—some three feet wide—were running in a zig-zag pattern. The gray jumping spiders, with thick, hairy legs, would go airborne, gliding as high as a castle turret and then landing with a thump. There were common black spiders too, with their eight bulging eyes, each looking around in a different direction. Very disturbing.

None were more feared than the black giant funnel-web spiders, who had large, red, puffy, pincer-like fangs hanging from their mouths. They had blood-red beady eyes and chompers able to bite small branches in half. Even small ones were known to leave very painful wounds.

Some of these hysterical and deranged beasts weighed over fifty pounds each. They moved low and fast for their size, hugging the ground with thick, black, hairy legs making the horrible, previously unidentified "pitter-patter, pitter-patter" sound.

Some extremely large tree branches were cracking under their weight. This was not good. The spiders came and just kept on coming. They stomped on everything in their path.

The prince did have the wherewithal to pull up his bow and arrow but then quickly realized his weapon would do little good. No arrow could stop thousands of spiders. He grabbed the Steward, threw her to the ground alongside a large log and covered them both with his mail surcoat. It was a heroic act by the prince.

The prince felt their furry, nasty appendages stepping on his head, his shoulders and his legs. They kept on screaming, poking and biting. They left gross drool on every surface they touched—sticky web-like strings of smelly, thick yucky. Some of the fatter ones sat on top of the prince, bounding up and down, poking and prodding. One sniffed and licked at his ears, which he tried to cover with his hands unsuccessfully.

It is hard to describe the sensation as the spider's prickly legs rubbed on the prince's exposed neck. They were hairy _and_ squishy—oh, and there are no words to describe the aroma. It was a combination of putrid, rank, whiffy, malodorous and foul. Just combine all those adjectives and let them sit in the hot August sun for a few hours, and you're about there. Oh, how he hated spiders.

It was one of the worst experiences of his life. And there was nothing he could do. He was as helpless as he could be. But he would not move off of the Steward. He felt responsible for her well-being.

The rampage went on for a long time, likely under an hour, but if you asked the prince, he would have said it went on and on. It was now just about an hour or so before dawn, and the early light was just beginning to layer upon the former dark darkness. The two slowly stood up from the log they hid behind, and they could finally see what happened.

The landscape was stripped bare. The trees had no leaves, and the grass was gone. They felt all over their bodies to see if either was hurt. Fortunately, while they were both covered with disgusting goo and smelled like—well, I just can't say in a polite audience—neither were wounded.

What few supplies they had—including their tents—were no more. Worst of all, the two were covered with yucky webbing, bites and just plain stickiness. The prince's chainmail and boots were also gone. His surcoat, once so regal and glorious, was in tatters. The coat of arms was barely discernible. Oh yes, remember the unhelpful broken sign? The only part left was the mysterious 'S' right at the prince's gooey feet.

"Spiders? Of course, the 'S' on the broken sign. 'Beware of Spiders.' Oh, I really hate spiders." The prince threw his hands in the air, frustrated with everything and disgusted with life itself.

Moments of abject silence passed. The Royal Steward knew to just be quiet.

"Well, we shouldn't stay here in this valley," the prince decided, feeling he should make a princely decision to protect the two of them. "They might come back. We also shouldn't start a fire. Perhaps fires set them off."

He pointed to a couple of large branches up in one of the few remaining trees. "Let's climb and wait until full daybreak."

That is exactly what they did. As he climbed, the prince noted the arachnid stickiness had gotten into his underclothes. Every time he moved an arm or a leg, the gluey substance painfully pulled at his skin and hair. It was so uncomfortable. Have you ever felt so dirty you couldn't think straight? "Toss good hygiene out the window with everything else," he bemoaned. "I can't even clean myself right anymore."

When he finally got to the branch he wanted, he leaned back on the tree and began to pick at all the goo. In short order, he had formed an orange-sized ball of gathered brownish mucilage.

Did you know certain bees go crazy at the smell of spider goo? Not many people do. The prince found out the hard way. It started with one buzzing, then two, and as quick as you can say 'spider goo,' hundreds of goo-crazed bees swarmed the prince. Since it wasn't quite dawn, he couldn't see them clearly, but he could sure hear them and feel their stingers.

He flailed his arms around his head attempting to swat some of them. But he slipped and fell off his high branch, hitting the hard ground and knocking the wind out of him. Still flailing his arms, he got up and ran toward the stream in the middle of the glen. He plunged in headfirst.

Unfortunately, for some unknown reason, the stream's water level had dropped during the spider onslaught. Maybe stampeding spiders get thirsty? Anyway, there was just a shallow trickle of water left surrounding a very embarrassed prince, face down in the mud—his bottom up in the air—swarming with relentless goo-crazy bees. The linen tunic and pants offered little protection.

By the time the bees calmed down, the prince had swollen whelps all over his back, face, arms and rear end—and of course, he was still covered with spider bites, goo and now cold, chilly mud. Yuck, yuck and more yuck.

Later, when the prince had a moment to finally look at his reflection in the water, it was disturbing. It turns out he was quite allergic to bee stings—or maybe spider bites—or both. Whatever the cause, his once-thin face had swollen twice its normal size. He looked like a pot-marked Mr. Potato Head with swollen red eyes.

Fortunately, the Royal Steward knew how to take the medicinal leaves she brought with her and make either a tasteless tea or a stinky poultice—she made both—and several of each. But healing would obviously take some time. The internal healing of the prince would take even longer.

The frustrated prince couldn't believe what had happened. Less than a week ago, he thought he could do just about anything. Now? He was beside himself.

[Storyteller's note: Can anyone tell me what 'beside himself' even means?]

These latest events just confirmed what the prince's critical inner voice was telling him. Even though he did his very best, his best wasn't good enough. Once again, he was another father's disappointment. He wasn't a princely prince. Everyone could see that. Certainly, the great King—who might be kind and even gracious—would have to agree in the end.

His critical inner voice was working overtime. "What were you thinking? You are not a prince. There are so many better choices. The great King deserved so much better."

The Royal Steward did her best to encourage the prince, but nothing helped. The despondent prince just knew the King would be disappointed. He was disappointed in himself.

The prince did imagine one silver lining. "Well, at least the worst is over." After what he'd experienced over the last three days, what more could the quest throw at him? Dragons, spiders, bees—oh my! At least now he can be a not-enough prince in peace.

But once again, he was wrong.

12

The Others

"It is not despair, for despair is only for those who see the end beyond all doubt. We do not."——Gandalf in J.R.R. Tolkien

The storyteller went on:

After only a day of recuperation, the prince regained some strength, though he hardly looked well. They decided to press on anyway.

He was a pitiful sight. With disgust, he looked down at his shredded surcoat over his soiled linen tunic and pants. His barely visible coat of arms, covered with spider goo and dirt, caused shame to envelop him.

They were able to purchase some old sandals for the prince from a traveling merchant. They didn't fit quite right, so he moved with a noticeable limp.

Walking south for maybe half a day, the weary travelers came across—drum roll, please—the Others. Their name doesn't cause fear to rise uncontrollably like the mention of other apex predators like grizzly bears, foxes, Godzilla, Bakugan Dragonoid Pyrus, or even Oz's flying monkeys, but in some ways, they are as harmful.

Maybe you have heard of emotional intelligence? EQ is the ability to sympathetically understand others because it's just a good thing to do. If you have a high EQ, you just seem to relieve relational stress around you and defuse conflict.

The 'Others' did just the opposite. Stress thrived in their wake. C'mon, we all have Others in our lives—often in our family. Do you remember the famous shout-out from Charlie Brown's Linus? "I love mankind; it's people I can't stand!!"—that's the Others.

Have you heard the other adage, "Some people are like birds; you help them fly and once they're in the air, they…well you know… on you." That's the Others.

You were probably told as a child, "Sometimes you need to learn to be quiet even when you have a lot to say." No one shared such basic wisdom with the Others.

Are you getting the idea? "It is hard to find a good listener." In the village of the Others, it is impossible.

The Others were self-focused, unsympathetic people who picked fights just because, and they just couldn't get any more inappropriate. The Others aren't burdened with sensitive hearts.

"Look, what have we 'ere?" said one of the larger, more condescending Others in a thick cockney accent with as much contempt as humanly possible.

By the way, most medium-level villains in true Quest tales speak cockney or some other British accent. According to a recent scholarly study of note, over 71.3% do. We will use this practice in our tale. No judgment to nice and respectable Brits. Back to the prince, who finds himself in a very precarious situation.

The prince guessed the large oppressive hulk was the leader of the Others, if they even have leaders.

"Hmmm, pretty coat of arms. Are you a prince of some sort?" The Other said as he pointed his thick finger toward the gooey mess on the prince's chest. The other Others just giggled and chuckled, knowing the fun was about to begin at the expense of these two pitiful-looking visitors.

The prince, despite feeling very unprincely at the moment, didn't back down. He stood up straight (as straight as his cheap flat sandals would allow) and proclaimed, "Aye, sirs and madams, that I am! I am the son of the great King." Even as he said it, he knew he didn't believe it himself. His whole stance deflated noticeably.

"Really? The great King?" said a tall, thin female Other with high poofy hair, emotionally baiting the prince even more. "'E's your father? Does 'e know you are out here wandering around, getting beat up by a couple of small dragons?" She emphasized 'small.' "Look, your pretty coat of arms is covered with dragon spit."

"Wait," said two aggressive twin female Others as they each grabbed one of Yeled's arms and pulled them apart to better see the gunked-up coat of arms.

"We love coat of arms riddles...such fun. It's like charades, isn't it, Gracie?" said the louder one. "Oh, no, Eleanor, you don't mean charades; you mean 20 questions, dear."

"Oh yes, of course, 20 questions. How silly of me!" chortled Eleanor. "Okay, Okay, what does mishpat mean?"

"Dearie, you have no idea how to play 20 questions, do ye? 'I spy with my little eyes something green.'"

An argument ensued between the two very large twins over which game they should play, all the while Yeled was getting tugged to and fro between them.

Finally, one Other cried out for the twins to cease and desist. He stepped out of the crowd with some confidence; obviously, he was one of the main Others. He was dressed like a cloaked guru of some kind, with beads, sandals, and a long walking stick he waved above his head. Yeled imagined he was a medicine man, priest or something like that.

"Silence! He is the keeper of COA magic."

He was just abbreviating "coat of arms."

"Oh, magic carrier," he continued, facing Yeled, "speak to us the riddle of the COA so we too can be successful and live happily ever after. Proclaim over us, 'mishpat, tzedakah, lipnay melek.' What does it all mean? We will listen."

"For your information, there is no magic here," the frustrated prince said. "Even if there were magic, I would not be the carrier. See?"

The Other shaman began to run around the front of the crowd, waving his hands in the air and yelling 'Mishpat, tzedakah, lipnay melek' over and over like it was some magic incantation.

"Shhhh! Here's the secret meaning," the prince added sarcastically. "They mean 'make whole,' 'do right for others' and 'be in the presence of the king.'" There, no more secrets. You are all officially so-be'd princes and princesses."

"And by the way," he pointed to the gook on the coat of arms, "not dragon spit—it's spider goo you ignorant Others. But how would you know? Spiders only swarm every century or so. They just happened to pick this year—the year of my quest—to do it."

The prince realized he was lecturing Others but couldn't seem to stop. "And as for the dragons I fought, they weren't small. I'd say definitely medium, and they were highly skilled and in very bad moods."

But as he thought about it, he couldn't be sure. How big do dragons get? Nomos hadn't discussed dragon sizes. Do they come in small, medium and large?

"What I mean to say," the prince said, trying to cover his hurt feelings, "yes, I think I remember there were perhaps some medium-sized dragons in the lot, but some big ones too—a couple very big. The bigger ones just got away before I could slay them properly."

Later, the prince would wonder if it was a good idea to defend himself to total strangers, to "Others." Once the spike of brain chemicals wore off, he realized there was nothing to be gained by convincing a single Other how big the dragons were. Convincing them of his enoughness was not part of his quest—that is, until now.

"Ooooh," one of the more overweight Other's swooned. "My, my, King-daddy will be soooo proud. This is your quest? Hey folk! Princie 'ere is on 'is quest."

The Other emphasized the word "quest" with a biting bit of deep mockery. "Yes, his quest. Oh my!" others echoed and shook their heads dismissively.

"Dada," said one tuft-headed young lad. "Dada, what's a quest?"

"Nothing, my boy, absolutely nothing," said a larger Other all too seriously. "Now go back home and do your chores, or yer mom and me will send you on one, and you'll end up looking like 'im."

The boy took one look at Yeled and ran through the crowd yelling, "MOMMY!"

"Hmmm," said the father. "The lad's right. It doesn't look like it is going well fer ya. We have seen other real princes, much larger ones, more princely, if you know what I mean, come through these woods."

The scoffing oozed out of the hairy Other.

"They looked...well, more prince-esque, to be sure. It looks like you wrestled with a beehive too. Not a smart idea for a real prince, am I right, boys?" He gibed the pitiful prince.

The other Others agreed and sneered and taunted him under their noticeably ripened breath. It didn't take long for the rest of the Others to pile on more derision, scorn, and mordacity. [I had to look up mordacity myself. It means biting.]

"And 'e's a bit skinny for a prince, don't you think?"

"And such a forthright nose. There could be a couple of princes in that snout."

"He could use a bath too. Didn't the last couple of princes have noticeably better hygiene?"

The prince had enough. He was still the prince after all—for a little while longer anyway. They would respect him, or he would make it so. He grabbed for the special royal sword at his side, only to remember it wasn't there anymore. "Dang, muffed it again," he thought to himself. "Maybe no one noticed?"

But they did.

"Look, 'ere! A prince with no sword. Ooooh, I don't think I have ever seen one of those, certainly not face-to-face," mocked another of the more overweight female Others.

You may remember Yeled losing his sword in the turbulent waters of a deep, raging river on the very first day of the quest—never to be found again. Well, back to the Others.

"Look, a swordless King wannabe," mocked another female Other. "What are you going to do to us, oh great, sword-challenged prince?

Poke your royal finger into our eyes. Beat us up with your sharp wit. Your stinkiness might just make us cry a little. What 'r your thoughts aboot hygiene? This is humiliating. One hopes for a better cut of royalty. Things aren't what they used to be in the Great Castle."

"Look, you buffoons," said Yeled, now frustrated and very angry. He held up his fists in a fighter's stance. Admittedly, he did look silly bouncing around, challenging the Others to a boxing match—one thin, emaciated bee-stung teen against dozens of big, brushy Others. It only made matters worse.

"I don't need a sword," bragged the prince. "Come on, let's go at it—fight like men—and, uh, large women."

The Others laughed and laughed at the pathetic young man.

Can I say one thing? It is likely obvious to you, no doubt, being the clever audience you are, the prince was not thinking princely—not at all. I am not judging. We have all been there. When we are challenged by Others, our brain releases a powerful fight-or-flight chemical making us either want to fight or run.

Oh, and there's more. The same chemical makes us unreasonable for at least three or four hours. It's brain science. No judgment of the prince. In a very short amount of time, he went from being a prince who heroically risked his own well-being to protect the Royal Steward from the horde of nasty spiders to...well this. People. What are you going to do?

Well, as you can guess, the prince's brain went into 'fight' mode. Bad choice. Looking at the sizes of the many Others, flight would have been a far better option. Ah, but remember, the prince was not being logical, not very princely either. He flung himself on the most vocal—and the largest Other.

The fight didn't go well for the prince. It didn't last long either before he was finally knocked to the ground.

The disdainful wisecracks went on and on and on and on. This is what the Others do, and they are good at it. All the prince could do was lay there, naked, under the onslaught of condescending comments.

Eventually, the Others just became bored and went about their day-to-day monotonous lives, looking for someone else they could emotionally beat up.

The prince was left devastated. The Others weren't the only voices telling him he wasn't enough. The critical dragon voice in his head had been saying the very same thing for years.

And now, for the first time, he became aware of something very disturbing. Most of the time, your inner voice is unmemorable and unrecognizable. Most often, it is your own voice. I suppose it is healthy, or at least normal.

Not this time. The prince recognized the dragon's voice in his head as his birth father's. "Boy, make us proud of you this time."

"Poppa, I can't," he muttered just before he passed out.

13

KICKING A MAN DOWN

"Buzz, Buzz, Buzz." Harvey realized his iPhone was ringing. He had only been at lunch for twenty minutes and hadn't even taken a bite of his sandwich yet. "Damn it. Back to work," he muttered.

Harvey looked at who was calling, hoping it wasn't yet another crisis. Could it get worse?

It was his sales manager, Sebastian, on the line. Sebastian had been with the company for about a decade and was critical to its success. Sebastian was easy to like and a good negotiator, though at times, he would favor customers who were his friends a little too much, thought Harvey. When the company was growing and the bottom line healthy, there was little impetus to criticize Sebastian's inefficiencies and quirks. However, these times were different.

"Hey boss," said Sebastian with a phony cheerfulness. No one has been very positive around the plant lately. "I need some advice on a client."

Sebastian rarely asks for advice; he excels at what he does. Harvey was more of a visionary entrepreneur, not a guy adept at small talk and cocktail parties. They are both comfortable in their unique roles but couldn't be more different.

"Sure, what's up?"

"Well, John Barr is canceling his orders this month. As I am sure you know, Barr Company represents about 15% of our monthly revenues. This cancellation is a huge hit."

"What...Why?" said Harvey, panic rising.

"Well, I went for drinks with John last night. He says the last few batches were not up to our old quality standards. He didn't say anything—you know—he's a friend and all—but he is taking his business elsewhere immediately."

"Quality? No one has a better record of quality than us," argued Harvey. "There isn't even a close second. What quality issues? I haven't heard of any issues. Sebastian, what the hell is going on?"

"Yeah, I had the same reaction, boss." Sebastian knew he was on the defensive. He must act quickly, or this conversation will not end well. "I checked with Sadie first thing. She didn't know about any quality issues either. She is as surprised as the rest of us."

"Well then, you are Barr's friend. What's going on?"

"My guess," said Sebastian as calmly as possible, "is they are hearing rumors of...well, you know... and want a safety net if..."

"If what?" barked Harvey.

Sebastian paused to make sure he chose the right words. "Well, you know, if our company goes down the tubes or has to lower our quality specs, or you...uh...retire or sell the company."

"Me, retire?" said a stupefied Harvey. "Where in the world did that come from? Sebastian, speak. Now!"

"Harvey, to tell you the whole truth," said Sebastian, knowing he couldn't avoid this any longer. "I have heard from other customers as well—three, maybe four—they are quite concerned about you and your age. Let's face it! You are this company. And it was your 69th birthday last month. Barr Company is young and has a long future ahead of it. It has to hook its chariot onto the latest winner, a growth company, a younger company with ideas and projects and a more forward-thinking approach to the business."

Harvey couldn't believe his ears. "We *are* forward-thinking, dammit. I built this place twenty years ago on forward-thinking. That hasn't changed. Who is saying we are not forward-thinking?"

Sebastian knew the conversation hadn't gone as well as he had hoped. He realized he should have done this in person. It might have gone better. Probably not.

"Old?" muttered Harvey, "Not forward thinking? No future?"

To his credit, Sebastian, usually not at a loss for words, said nothing.

Dejected and equally at a loss for words, Harvey wanted to say, "Thanks for the heads-up!" However, what came out surprised even him. "Look, Sebastian, you are the sales guy. Fix this, or you can join Dwayne, the genius, at his new, younger, forward-thinking company." He hung up the phone unceremoniously.

Harvey was beyond upset. He was enraged. His pulse rose noticeably—even he felt it. He took a couple of deep breaths to calm down, then some more. Had he become that guy—the guy he had never thought he would be—old, a business discard, out of good ideas that others would want and appreciate, like a fish sitting on a pier in the sun for too long? He didn't see it coming. Not at all. Who else knew and wouldn't tell him to his face? What were the others thinking?

He took a few deep breaths and decided to go to Scooter's tonight. He wasn't sure why, but he needed to do something. Something had to change.

He knew he needed to chill some before he went back to work. His heart rate was sky-high. If El were here, she would demand that he lay down. But she wasn't, and Harvey wasn't sure where she was. He missed her but didn't quite know how to communicate that—part of the problem, he supposed.

The book. Of course, why not? A few moments of irresponsibility in 50 years seems reasonable. He was due. And, like the book said, "Could it get any worse?" He was afraid this time the answer would be 'yes.'

Nevertheless, he decided to turn the page to the next chapter, The Beginning of the End.

"Maybe the book was listening. It's weird. I wonder what the prince would do in my place. Well, he has his problems to deal with—a heck of a lot of them. Something has to turn things around, right? It's a book for adolescents. You know something happens, and they all live happily ever after. He'd better hurry. He's running out of chapters. C'mon boy, step up."

14

THE BEGINNING OF THE END

The storyteller went on:

Yeled strained to open his eyes. They were dusty and dry as if he had swum through an old sand dune in the blisteringly hot Sahara Desert without goggles. Kids don't try this at home.

He tried to shake the cobwebs out of his head, but everything hurt—his neck, his arms, and even his earlobes. How do you hurt your earlobes? The prince did. There was also a sharp ache in his left side, and he couldn't breathe very well—maybe a broken rib or two? He had been in a real battle. He just couldn't remember what happened.

Sometimes loss of memory is the result of a big fight. Your brain just covers it up for a while, as it is designed to protect you from being hurt—in this case, the memory of getting hurt.

Don't worry, the prince will be okay. It just takes some care, some time, and lots of liquids and sleep. This was way before Advil was created.

Just before he fell back to sleep, he asked, "Where am I?"—well, actually, just an incomprehensible mumble. It sounded more like "weeerummereyehmmm?" His heavy eyelids leaned shut as he drifted back into a dark, hopefully healing sleep.

The next thing he remembered was waking up again. The room was still dark, except for a single light off to his right side. He realized he wasn't alone. And it wasn't just a light; it was a torch, a blazing torch coming closer and closer and someone with big hands and thin, long fingers holding it.

He tried to determine who or what phantom was hidden behind the flame. He couldn't tell. Maybe one of the Others?

Oh, the Others—he remembered now—the Others and the fight. And how badly he had handled the whole thing.

Fear struck deep in his soul. Not just any fear, Yeled was terrified.

"Who's there?" Yeled croaked out, urgently looking around, trying to see where the threats were. "Tell me. Who are you?" he demanded. "Speak or fight."

"Son..." the voice echoed eerily behind the torch, sounding more like a slow, wraithlike moan. "Son," it slowly repeated, "make me proud...this time...this time. Don't be a disappointment again. Do you hear me, boy?"

"Poppa. Da', is it you?" Yeled couldn't believe it. It was his dad's words, but not his voice, and his dad had perished in the coup years ago.

"Why didn't you make me proud, boy?" The specter continued, not in response to Yeled's question and showing no interest in what Yeled

had to say. "It's all your fault. Do you hear me, boy? You shamed me. You will never belong...ever."

Yeled's stomach felt nauseous. Sweat beaded on his cold forehead. He was having a panic attack. He couldn't move. He grabbed a few quick breaths, but it didn't help.

He was confused, frightened and struggled to slow his breathing when another voice erupted—not a voice but a screeching. "You don't deserve to be a prince, do ya? You know, don't you?" howled a vile female character with a thick, unpolished brogue, standing just off to the left of the torch holder. She was moving slowly toward him, only a couple of feet away now.

"Yer a fake. That's what you are," said a little child's voice to the right of the flame.

"Everyone knows your dark secret," screeched a guttural voice, emphasizing the word "dark." Someone cackled just behind them. "Yer foolin' no one. Everyone can see what you see."

Now all the entities were moving closer, surrounding him. He could do nothing to stop them. He was drowning in the vile swamp of downward gazes. The creatures began to swirl in the air about him, berating him with more and more accusations.

"It is the King who is the most embarrassed," said the voice holding the bright torch. "He stood up for you. And just look at you now! We all deserve so much better than you. You know who you are," the voice paused. "You're your father's son."

Then, as if on cue, the light shifted, and he could at last see their faces. He blinked desperately, trying to make sense of it all. It was the Others, and they were striking the ground with their pitchforks, axes, and hoes, thumping in a loud, eerie rhythm, bang, bang, bang. In between the striking, the vile crowd, in unison, cried out, "Fake!"

Bang... "Fake!"

Bang... "Fake!"

Bang... "Fake!"

The light shifted again, and what he saw took his breath away—not the faces of Others. All the men, women, boys, and girls, each to a person, had his face—hundreds of Yeleds staring back at him!

He tumbled to the ground on all fours and wept uncontrollably.

Harvey was shocked by this chapter. "Damn, the book has taken a dark turn. But I guess teens today are used to stuff like this. Too bad."

But this heavy emotional stuff reminded Harvey of conversations with his counselor, well, one of the last four. He remembered. It was the lady with the nose ring and pink hair. Not that that bothered him. It was just how he remembered her.

She might have been the best of the four and would have called this big-time daddy issues. The poor kid was subconsciously still trying to earn his dead father's favor. How's he going to do that? It's hard enough with a live father—but a dead one?

"Whew," Harvey thought to himself. "Might as well head back to the Others and get some sage advice." He chuckled at his own joke.

"I want to get a bit further before going to Scooters tonight," he thought. "So, it's going to be an hour-long lunch. Let someone complain. Just like Ralph said in *The Honeymooners*, 'Pow, right in the kisser.'"

What's the next chapter? The Beguiler. Wow, dragons, spiders, bees, Others, dead parents, and now, a beguiler? Hmmm," Harvey thought to himself. "Let me Google it."

He pressed a few buttons on his cell phone, and there it was, "Beguiler, someone who leads you to believe something that is not true."

"Exactly what I was trying to tell Sebastian. Someone's setting me up. It's all lies. So, yep, this could be a very informative chapter," he silently mused and began to read the Tale of the Unlikely Prince, chapter ten, The Beguiler.

15

THE BEGUILER

When the prince awoke again, he was back in bed—though definitely not his own. His head was still pounding, and though his wounds were dressed, his whole body still ached beyond words. It took a few moments for him to begin to regain the use of his mental faculties, no doubt due to the complete beating he took at the hands of the Others.

He remembered, and it caused shame to boil up again. He should have known better. A true prince would not have let the Others get under his skin. Once more, Yeled proved to the entire world he just wasn't prince enough—certainly not worthy of the King's respect and honor. What in the world is he going to say to the King when he sees him? Or Nomos?

He uttered a deep, deep sigh—you know the kind—it's what someone naturally does who is just totally defeated and can't see a way forward. He breathed in and exhaled again, still not feeling even a little bit better. He could only lift his head—gently, oh, so gently. He had never felt so much pain.

The prince considered getting up out of bed, gently setting one leg on the floor and then the other but thought better of it after he felt shooting pain down his side and even more dizziness. He decided the wise thing was to just lie there for a while, maybe a few minutes until he felt he could manage life again. Maybe the Steward will show up with some of the special tonic she kept with her for such aches and pains. She was quite skilled and her tonics were very effective.

"Wait a minute, the Steward," he thought to himself. "Where might she be?" He realized she was nowhere to be seen. Wherever he was, he was alone. Even more curious, he thought.

Then, like a nasty, painful retching, the memories of the nightmare boiled into his brain, causing him to shudder again. You know, sometimes you have dreams, and upon waking, you can't remember what happened at all. They just disappear into the darkness like a mist. Not this time. Sometimes nightmares can be good, but most are not.

[Storyteller's note: I have this nightmare of being chased around my house by a purple dog with no teeth and very bad breath. Yuck.]

I digress once more.

The prince wished he could just forget the nightmare, yet he seemed to recall every ugly detail: the mysterious floating torch, the Others, his father's hands and everyone's face morphing into his own—or maybe they were always his.

Even though his brain said it wasn't real—it couldn't be real, right? It still caused him to recoil with deep apprehension.

He paused and thought, "Maybe it was real." After all, everything was such a jumble in his head. How could he be sure of what's real and what's not? If he was going mad, how would he even know? Don't insane people truly think they are rational? In psychiatric hospitals all over the kingdom, you can find people who are 100% sure they are Joan of Arc, Moses, or a duck. And they are totally at peace with their 'truth.'

These dangerous thoughts made Yeled convulse violently, but since he hadn't eaten for a long time, he just became more and more nauseous. "Oh, where was the Steward?" he thought.

"Enough!" he said aloud to no one at all. Even if it hurt, he didn't want to just keep lying there, having the nightmare keep bouncing around his skull over and over. He needed to do something, even if he didn't feel like it. But what?

He paused and looked around the huge bedroom. In front of him was an ornate picture window, maybe fifteen feet high. Halfway up the sky, a fuzzy, pale orb was trying to burn its way through the thick fog blanketing the valley. "The sun will soon burn through the shadowy vale, and I hope it will warm things up," Yeled imagined.

Little did he know this particular valley remained quite dark most of the time.

Even so, the view of the sun attempting to rise gave him a moment of hope and familiarity. His stomach relaxed a little, and the nightmare's vile fingers released their stranglehold on him for now.

Yeled decided to take advantage of the respite and at least visually explore his surroundings.

The bed he was lying in was magnificent, quite plush, not your typical straw-filled variety he was used to at the castle. This luxurious four-poster bed exuded an air of opulence, royalty and comfort. The bed frame was massive, crafted from rich, dark wood adorned with intricate carvings. The four tall posts rose from each corner of the bed, reaching towards the high ceiling, embellished with lovely decorative finial caps.

Yeled had never seen anything close to this extravagance, even in the highest chambers of the King's palace.

As a matter of fact, this bed was worthy of a king—no, a great king. The headboard and footboard were generously padded and upholstered in sumptuous fabrics; it looked like velvet, silk, or some combination, featuring intricate embroidery of knights and other warriors defeating dragons of all kinds.

"Where in the world am I?" thought Yeled again as he quietly gazed about the spacious bedroom. "Whose house could this be? Or palace?"

Though he wanted to get up and explore some more, he still couldn't get out of bed—not just yet. "Maybe if I just lay down for a few more minutes." So he gently placed his throbbing head on the pillow. And instantly, his life was changed.

Well, it's a bit of an overstatement, but the pillow. Look, the prince has slept in a variety of beds, for sure, but nothing matched the dramatic softness he felt when his tired head lay down on this pillow. Most people in the Kingdom had straw-filled beds. They weren't comfortable, particularly the pillows, but hey, straw was readily available. If you had a little savings, you might upgrade to horsehair pillows and mattresses. They are comfortable too, I suppose.

You know, I have always wanted to ask someone where they get all the horsehair. I will have to do some scholarly research and get back to you.

Some of the highest echelon of sleepers prefer down feathers from ducks or geese, but it costs an arm and a leg to get fifty pounds of feathers. Comfortable? Oh yes, you might be surprised.

But this pillow? This pillow was far superior to all of those. Yeled couldn't even find the words to describe what he was experiencing—a "feathery haven of comfort." "Utter bliss to touch and squeeze." It was "so sculptable and, yes, huggable even." Did you know high-end manufacturers measure the moldability of luxury pillows? Moldability refers to how easily the pillow can be shaped or scrunched. The prince's head now rested on a very moldable pillow. It clearly was not manufactured by some machine, no. It was hand-fluffed by someone who knew what hand-fluffing was all about. And of course, the pillow was naturally hypoallergenic. Can a pillow be euphoric? If so, this one was. Yes, surely the best pillow he'd ever experienced.

"What is going on?" he asked himself again as he scrunched the pillow for the fourth time. "Did the King's bed feel like this?" Yeled wondered, still quite distracted.

It was not just the pillow. The prince also noted the bed had a massive canopy made up of sheer and flowing fabrics, creating a warm and dreamy ambiance. The room was also amply provided with expensive complementary furniture pieces, nightstands, dressers, and seating arrangements mirroring the bed's opulence.

And that's not all; his tattered princely clothes, each embroidered with the coat of arms, were noticeably missing. But he was wearing an exquisite, brushed wool nightshirt. Very comfy. It was the most comfortable nightshirt he had ever known.

All this opulence only raised the prince's curiosity. Pain or no pain, he needed answers. "Hello? Hello?" The prince tried to vocalize, but it only came out as a gravelly whisper. "Hello, where am I?" his voice croaked inaudibly.

He tried to speak louder, but his voice was still frustratingly weak.

After some more time struggling to get someone's attention, he heard a sound from what he assumed was a hallway outside his closed door. Steps were coming his way, not in a rush or in any way threatening. Just someone casually coming down the hall.

His door slowly cracked open, and an older man, about the King's age, the prince estimated, stuck his well-coifed, gray-bearded head in the door opening. He smiled broadly and comfortingly and began speaking to the prince.

"Oh, say hello there, young prince. May I come in?" The older man inquired with an upper-class British accent, likely from Surrey or Buckinghamshire. The prince nodded cautiously but did not try to get up from the bed again.

"Welcome to my home. My name is Dolos. I am the lord of this castle. I imagine you have a lot of questions. In time, all will be answered. First, I want you to feel safe. You are under my protection and enjoy my hospitality. Fortunately, I was out hunting by the road this afternoon. I heard a ruckus and saw the Others shamefully beating the tar out of you. I think you were very brave, yet I must say, the fight was ill-advised even for someone of your stature and skill. I chased them off with my bow and arrows and brought you here. Only as I began to dress your wounds did I recognize you as the prince. Welcome to my fiefdom, my prince. What is mine is yours." Dolos bowed respectfully.

The respectful bow felt really good to the prince, especially after the cheeky and discourteous treatment he had received from the Others, not to mention the dragons and the spiders. It felt almost as wonderful and scrunchable as the pillow. The prince smiled a little. He couldn't remember when he had smiled last.

"Please tell me, O great prince, why are you so far from the King's castle? These are dangerous woods. I don't mean anything by my comment; it's nothing derogatory. I mean, well, a great prince like you should be leading a great army, a great consort made up of great warriors mirroring his bravery and glory."

The prince thought about it a bit and agreed. Lord Dolos' logic did make a lot of sense. What was he really doing out here?

"The truth?" confessed the prince matter-of-factly. "I was on my official quest, Lord Dolos. I went out from the castle to earn the glory you speak of. Yet I failed miserably, again and again. I have concluded that no matter how hard I try, I am not a great prince, not at all."

As he spoke, the prince, ignoring the constant pain, carefully rolled up to a sitting position on the luxurious bed and planted his naked feet gently on the exotic hardwood floor—maybe rare Zebra wood, he thought.

He was a pitiful sight, really, so filled with shame and self-contempt. He wouldn't, no, he couldn't look into the gracious eyes of his host.

"Oh, young prince, may it never be so," said Dolos as he walked around to stand right in front of the prince, making sure to look directly into the prince's eyes. "You are a prince! I have gazed upon your coat of arms. That is enough for all to see you as a person to whom honor is due. Those men and women in the village should never have treated you so. They are a horrible lot. Why, I am surprised—please do not take offense at my words—your stepfather allowed you to go out alone, without an armed escort worthy of your rank."

Yeled was still too confused and in such pain to realize Dolos had spoken of his stepfather, the King. If Yeled were at the top of his game, he might have realized there is more to Dolos than meets the eye. How could a stranger possibly know about his relationship with the King? But Yeled was far from the top of his game.

"Please, young friend, rest up," Dolos continued graciously with a wide, disarming smile. "Later tonight, we will have a feast for you—a grand banquet worthy of a prince of real substance and glory. I will send you a servant. He was my son's servant before my sole heir's untimely death a few years ago."

Dolos clearly struggled to speak of his late son as he paused to wipe a tear from his eyes. It is painful to lose a child, no doubt. Or was it something else? You decide.

"My servant, Momos," said Dolos as he pointed to a man standing at the door. Bald, thin, and standing quite erect, Momos was dressed in a black formal suit with very little expression on his face. "He will serve you well. You can trust him."

Yeled just couldn't believe his fortune finally. No dragons, spiders, bees, or even Others. He just wasn't used to being treated so well. And yet, something was bothering Yeled.

"Excuse me, sir, uh, Lord Dolos," Yeled quietly inquired. "I was traveling with a companion, a woman. Is she here as well? Have you seen her?"

"Ah yes, she was here, of course, and was taking good care of you for a time. She wanted me to tell you she has gone back to the castle for some special medicines, fresh clothes, and other assorted sundries. She said not to worry. She will be back as soon as she can. I even gave her a fast horse and an escort just to make sure she was safe. But she strikes me as someone who can take care of herself, eh?"

This surprised Yeled a little. Until this moment, he would have never thought the Royal Steward would leave him for any reason. Her charge, which she was very faithful to, was to support him in his quest. But maybe it makes sense. She is coming back after all. He could use fresh clothes, he supposed.

"Thank you, Lord Dolos, for your care and generosity," said Yeled as he attempted to stand once more, his head still pounding. "I am sure all is well."

"Please lay back down, son," said Dolos as he reached out and grabbed Yeled's shoulders for support. "You are in no shape to get out of bed yet. Allow my faithful servant, Momos, to fix you a tonic for your headache and bruised ribs. He is a miracle worker, to be sure."

Yeled did just that.

Are your red flags going up too?

Maybe I can offer you a free trip to an inclusive resort in Cancun—no strings attached? Or scenic swampland in Louisiana for just a handful of dollars. Or the good news that a total stranger in a distant land has passed away and left you as the recipient of his entire estate.

As one wise guy once said, "If a story sounds too good to be true, it's probably sold out."

Harvey's red flags were not only up; they were waving. "Run, kid, run," he thought to himself. "He's not your father!"

Harvey couldn't stop now, so he continued to the next chapter.

16

THE SHOCKING QUESTION

T he storyteller went on:

At dinner, Yeled got to know more about his host. Dolos was a substantial man, a very wealthy farmer, with cattle beyond count, even a small army at his disposal, and fields farmed by innumerable servants. Not as great as the prince's stepfather, to be sure; however, Dolos' stature was on the larger side of expansive nonetheless.

Over the next few days, the prince began to heal—outwardly, of course, but more notably, inwardly—or so it seemed to him. His host was more than gracious. All that belonged to him and his late son was indeed laid before the prince. They dined, drank, and smoked pipes together. Kids don't try this at home; it is a filthy habit. Yeled will regret it, to be sure.

They told each other great stories—some real, some, shall we say, embellished—and laughed until the prince could laugh no more. Dolos truly seemed to relish Yeled's stories about the dragons and spiders he encountered. Dolos hated bees just about as much as Yeled; in fact, they seemed to have a great deal in common. Dolos never made fun of Yeled's failures, never sought to give advice, nor even showed judgment.

"Brave prince," affirmed Dolos. "It is to your great credit you survived the spider stampede. How horrible! I know of no one else who has. And you risked your own well-being by throwing your body on top of your companion. That was a purely heroic act few would attempt. She is alive because of you, no doubt. You are probably too humble to say so, but I will. You are a hero."

This felt very different from the response he expected from the King. Yeled was beginning to feel valued, appreciated and even respected. So, it didn't take long for him to open up even more about his family in Garden City, the tragic calvary charge, and the so-be'd adoption to the King.

"Ah," said Dolos, making a sweeping gesture with his hand. "I am very familiar with Garden City. I remember at one point in time, the garden there was very lush and wonderful—until it all came crashing down—not anyone's fault really. It is all too bad and highly preventable, uh...at least what I heard."

"Son, I am also so sorry about the calvary charge. But you were only 15, and you were doing the will of your parents. It's not your fault, don't you see? You were dealt a very bad hand. I am sure your father didn't really mean what he said: 'Son, make us proud of you this time.' Heat of the moment stuff, I suspect. Do you miss them?"

The question took Yeled aback, and he had to think before he answered. Did he miss his mother and father? No one had asked him such a thing before. All he knew was he had been such a disappointment to them. So, did he miss them? He would say he wished he could go back and do it all over again—better—so he could finally hear his father praise him and brag to his friends about his exploits and character. That is the deepest desire of his wounded heart, even to this day. But it will never be.

Dolos listened to Yeled's story with seemingly great interest and even greater empathy. "My boy, I have no doubt your father was proud of you. I would be if I were your father."

That last statement shocked Yeled, but he was not sure why. I will tell you it was a foreshadow of things to come.

"Have I told you about my son?" Dolos asked Yeled. "He would be about your age. I loved him so much—more than you can imagine. I have no doubt you would be besties with him. He was fun, smart, courageous, competitive and compassionate. Every day, I told him what I thought of him. 'Son, I just want to tell you how proud I am to be your father. I can't wait to see the man you are going to become and what you will accomplish. I would buy stock in you. There is nothing you could ever do to make me ashamed to be your father.'"

Yeled couldn't believe his ears. Did such a father-son relationship exist? Really? Why had he been dealt such a bad hand? It was like he got a 7-2 off-suit Texas Hold'em poker hand. No one wins with such a bad hand, no matter how you play it. While you can bluff in playing cards, it is much harder in real relationships.

Yeled had to admit to himself he was a bit jealous of the relationship Dolos had with his late son—no, he was very jealous. That is all he ever wanted. So much more than the quest even.

Lord Dolos's wife, Apatê, was also more than kind. She sewed the prince's torn clothes and presented them to him as almost new. She even polished his great shield. It shone like the sun. He thanked her profusely and put them both away in the old pine bureau in the corner of their deceased son's room. He wasn't sure he would need them anymore.

Yeled felt quite—what's the right word?—venerated here. Loved, accepted, honored and secure. And, by the way, the scrunchable superior pillow didn't hurt.

A few weeks passed. Yeled couldn't believe he had been there so long already and missed the King less and less. Thoughts about the quest were rarer still. One evening, at dinner, Dolos popped the question to Yeled.

"My son," began Dolos. *Yeled had resisted the compliment those times Lord Dolos accidentally called him "my son." But no longer. He actually longed to hear it.*

"I have no right to ask you this, so please do not be offended in any way. I am a lonely man with a vast empty house and no heir. Apatê and I just can't stop talking about how well you fit into our household, or dare I say, our family. It is as if my late son has come home."

"And your friend has not returned for you. I can keep sending scouts to find some answers, but you may not want to hear them. You yourself said if you ever returned to the castle, you would be facing only shame and contempt. I couldn't bear such shame for you. You don't deserve it."

"And listen, the impossible quest your stepfather gave you was too much. Inevitably, you would fall short—anyone would. In fact, you did everything you could possibly do—and yet, what are the chances your former stepfather would ever give you your rightful due? In his presence, you just aren't enough for some reason. You deserve so much more, my son. May I speak openly? You should not even need a quest to prove your worth to anyone. All can see it. I can see it. Apatê sees it. I am rambling." *Dolos paused as if to gather his thoughts.* "Look, would you consider becoming my son? I can't imagine a greater honor than becoming your stepfather. What do you say?"

Certainly, boys and girls, you can see through my gimmick of narrative parallelism. Two adoptions, two sons, two stepfathers—similar in some ways but far different in others. Let me elaborate. In the first instance, the unlikely prince was adopted by fiat into the family of the great King pending a successful quest (or so Yeled thought). In the second case, the failed prince is now being offered a "new and better" adoption—sans-quest. Interesting?

Well, the prince was surprised at the unexpected offer. No judgment from me. I get it. But surely, you've heard the old adage, "If it's too good to believe, it likely is." Are you noticing something non-kosher here? Hold on to those thoughts.

Yeled wondered to himself. "Is it true? Finally, a father who actually adores me, who sees my true potential, who understands what I have gone through, who has my back? This is the favor of a father I have longed for—my whole life—and no need for a nasty quest to earn it? Is this even possible?"

Alas, the prince didn't take very long at all to consider the offer. Why delay? He couldn't recall ever being happier. Dolos was the father he never had—and always longed for. Was this what being a son was supposed to feel like? Lord Dolos never criticized Yeled and never showed disappointment. If he were honest, Yeled had come to prefer Dolos over his stepfather, the Great King—though out of residual respect for his former liege, he would never say that out loud.

The way Yeled figured it, if he agreed to Dolos' request and became his son, this would put this regretful quest to bed for good. "Good riddance," Yeled thought. He had messed up the quest big time. He had not acted princely—not enough, to be sure. Also, if he accepted, he would never have to face the King's disappointment. Or Nomos'. Both would hurt way too much.

It's funny how our minds will play tricks on us. The prince remembers his former stepfather saying, "This quest will bring to you an experience of the favor you long for, dear prince." Of course, you and I know the King didn't say this—not even close. Memory can be a squirrelly thing, skilled at morphing if need be. Such was the case here. We are all experienced justifiers of our own actions. This proficiency is not limited to princes. In the prince's mind, Dolos' love for him was the real deal. It required no quest, no hoops to jump through, nothing more. The prince could be himself at last. That made him smile.

The prince agreed to become Dolos' son and wanted to do it as soon as possible.

To make things even sketchier, Yeled even justified not sending a messenger to the King informing him of his decision and the quest's ignominious end. "After all," he made the case in his head: "The King is a long way from here, and what has he done to come find me? Nothing. I am doing him a favor really. Why cause the King more concern and disappointment? What is over is over."

But is it?

17

Not Always What They Appear

The storyteller went on:

At last, the great adoption day arrived. No expense was spared, an affair filled with a great deal of pomp and circumstance. People came from all over the valley. There was laughter, singing and other revelry I will not go into right now. Suffice it to say, everyone was having a grand time. Even Yeled.

Apatê had altered their son's royal garment to fit Yeled. Yeled was about the same size in the shoulders and the waist but was four inches taller. She had done a very professional job.

At the appointed time, Yeled stood before the grand thrones of Lord Dolos and Lady Apatê and kneeled.

Dolos stood over the humble prince and waved his hands over the vast audience, proclaiming, "Today, my son has been restored.

Of course, not him, but in the guise of another great knight, Prince Yeled.

The crowd cheered, "Huzzah, huzzah, huzzah for Lord Dolos and His new son Yeled."

Once more, Dolos waved his arms to silence the crowd. To commemorate this event, Apatê had gone to great expense to restore Yeled's great sword which had fallen into disrepair during his quest. He turned to Apatê, took the huge sword from her, and walked back over to Yeled.

"My new son, it is my great privilege to knight you, Sir Yeled." He dipped the shining sword onto Yeled's right shoulder and began to switch to his left.

But something struck Yeled like lightning. "Wait a minute," he said with great concern in his voice as Dolos was lowering the sword to Yeled's other shoulder.

"What is this? My sword? It cannot be. My sword was lost on the first day of my quest. It fell into the rapids and could never be found. What is this? What is happening? Wait..."

In a millisecond, to Yeled's shock, everything changed; the entire celebration just seemed to melt away into black nothingness. The crowd was violently absorbed into a dark void, along with the castle and all the rest of the pomp and splendor. Now it was just Yeled, all alone with Dolos and Apatê. Finally, he could see they were also not what they appeared to be.

Surrounded by other-worldly shadows, Yeled watched helplessly as Dolos morphed into a horrible, bent-over, aged man with long, stringy red hair and a severe, hoary face. His eyes lost all their light and were surrounded by sinister dark scars making his mishappened forehead even more disturbing. He seemed to grow to twice his usual size, and now Yeled could see his face was encompassed by a multitude of repulsive black serpents with poisonous mouths bared.

Then, as fast as a snake strike, Dolos' pale hand shot out and grabbed Yeled's exposed neck. His inflamed, contorted fingers, much stronger than Yeled imagined, instantly wrapped around his neck and started to choke him. With surprisingly little effort, Dolos lifted Yeled off the ground. All Yeled could do was flail around impotently, hopelessly trying to pry open the steely death grip.

"You foolish boy," said Dolos with an ugly sneer, drawing as close as he could to Yeled's reddening face, his voice oozing with cruelty. "There truly is no place for someone like you who was given so much and appreciated it so little. What the King..." Dolos said, spitting on the ground as if he couldn't bear to say the epithet. "What he sees in you, I cannot imagine. Before I take what pathetic shred of life you have away from you, let me introduce myself. I am Dolos, the son of my father, Darkness. I am known by other names, such as Mendacius and the Lord of trickery, falsehood, and lies.

My brothers and sisters, you might also know quite well: Fear, Envy, Anger, Unfaithfulness and Complaint. I told you I was familiar with Garden City. I will add I was intimately—if I may say so—familiar with your pathetic parents too. They, like you, despised the gifts given to them and just couldn't stop longing for more. Deceiving them was far too easy.

And you? You wanted to be deceived. Like they say, the tree doesn't grow far from the apple, if you understand my meaning.

"Boy!" Dolos now growled like some feral animal, his eyes turning ugly yellow. "Do you want to hear a little joke?" He laughed derisively. "It turns out you are just like your father.

It's the definition of irony, of course. In the end, he was not one to count on. He thought so little of everyone. He was never satisfied with the status quo. Always blaming others for his misfortunes. Your mother, too. True, they had their own issues. I will tell you a little secret. They were so easy to manipulate. Oh, and they loved pillows too."

Dolos continued to squeeze Yeled's frail neck harder and harder. Yeled's brain screamed at the beginning pangs of oxygen deprivation. His eyes rolled back in his head. In the end, all he could hear was the vile victory laughter of Dolos and the ugly cackling of his hateful bride, Apatê.

"Enough, foul imp," a voice familiar to Yeled rang out in the din. The voice was very loud and without any inkling of fear. "Release him...or else, Serpent. You have no authority to harm him. This one is of the King."

Dolos, caught unaware by the unexpected challenge, looked around to see the source. He recognized her immediately, of course. This wasn't the first time they had tangled. Though he would never show it or admit it, he couldn't help but tremble in fear.

Standing behind him, and about a foot shorter, was a thin, erect black woman, her gray hair wildly unfurled and her hands raised aggressively into the skies. It was the Royal Steward. Yeled was totally shocked at her appearance. Gone were the warm, compassionate eyes and gentle smile. Her face was filled with rage—the countenance of a great warrior. She stood in Dolos' face as one with unimaginable authority, and Dolos knew it.

Whatever his game, it was over.

Realizing the battlefield had shifted, Dolos begrudgingly set Yeled on the ground, though his age-spotted cold fingers still held firm on Yeled's neck.

"Noomai, you are too late. He is mine." Dolos barked at her with great contempt, though perhaps some apprehension as well. When such evil is faced with a far greater power, it must shake in its boots. It has no real Plan B.

It is surprising what the human brain does under oxygen deprivation. Yeled was shocked he had never asked the Royal Steward's name.

Dolos continued, sounding a bit more desperate now, like a career prosecuting attorney arguing another losing case. "Woman, this one's relationship to the King is now forfeit. He is my son. He agreed to my terms. Go ahead, ask him." He pointed arrogantly at the boy with his free hand. "The King's law, you see, is on my side. This pathetic boy is mine to do whatever I so desire."

Dolos smiled a most despicable smile and spit on the ground again.

Children, spitting is such a nasty habit. Don't do it. It's disrespectful and quite unsanitary. You are better than that—back to the story.

Then, Noomai's eyes lit up like two grand, unquenchable bonfires, and her countenance inflamed like a great flaming star.

"You abominable deceiver. Isn't it enough you are allowed for a time to roam around the valleys and do your destruction? And yet you still seek to challenge the King and undermine his will. Have you never learned your place? Your arrogance is beyond measure. You have no authority here." Noomai flicked her hand like she was disposing of some nasty bug.

"This one is of the King and that will never change. Your claims are worth their weight in sheep dung. Release him now. Any delay is to your own peril."

Knowing once again he had fallen short and was defeated, Dolos snarled and released Yeled roughly. Yeled collapsed on the hard ground, gasping for air. Dolos, not daring to take his eyes off the Royal Steward, turned one last time to spit on the coughing Yeled.

"We are not done, you self-righteous witch," barked Dolos, pointing his white finger directly at her face—a pathetic final challenge of little weight at all. He was far outmatched and knew it. "You and I will have it out eventually. You'd best watch your back."

The Royal Steward just laughed out loud at the meaningless threat. She too was of the King and wielded his power. She relaxed a little, setting her arms gently at her side, and prophesied.

"Snake, in the end, you will wear out like a garment, like a thin, flimsy robe; you will just be rolled up and tossed like the rest of the trash into the fire and burned."

Yeled opened his eyes again, just in time to witness something remarkable—no, something miraculous. The Royal Steward rose on her tiptoes and reached up, grabbing the very corners of the world, and rolled it up like it was a beat-up old stage backdrop—Dolos, Apatê, the castle, the entire valley, the whole thing—and just kicked it aside.

Well, I didn't see that coming. Did you? Is this exciting, or what?

"Yeah, good for the Royal Steward. Ata girl," thought Harvey, really getting into the story. "She saved the prince's bacon for sure."

He looked again at how much of the book he still had to read. Only a few chapters were left; this was a terrible place to stop. But it was time to return to the real world, with real-world Others, snakes, and many beguilers.

Harvey tossed the rest of his lunch in the trash bin—he could never figure out what was recycle and what was trash, so he just threw it all in one of the holes.

The moment he stepped into his office, he was immersed in yellow Post-it notes, phone calls to return, and those he needed to make to save the business—it was all too much. He longed for some good news, but the day only brought more disappointments, leaving him feeling isolated and defeated.

Harvey was hurting and utterly alone.

18

SCOOTERS PLACE

"Harvey, great to have you here," said Scooter, surprised to see Harvey at his door. It was drizzly out, so some regulars had taken rain checks. "I wasn't sure you would come. Come on in. I think you know the guys and their wives. I invited the whole gang. It's pretty much a full house."

Scooter was also one of Harv's golf regulars. Five others were there—all professionals in business of some kind. Their ages ranged from mid-40s to, well, Harvey. All were from the same church, too.

"Harvey, let me introduce you to our guest of honor, Dr. McClellan," Scooter said with a warm smile. "Ben and I go way back. We've had many deep conversations about faith and life over the years, and his insights about God's love for the unlovable in particular have always been enlightening."

Dr. Ben McClellan was a short, grey-headed, grandfatherly, and professorial-looking gentleman. He wore an old English smoking jacket with a houndstooth pattern and leather-reinforced elbows. Harvey thought all that was missing was a Sherlock Holmes pipe. Harvey's eyes widened, and he thought, "It's Nomos!"

"Dear Harvey, please call me Ben," said Ben charmingly.

Dr. McClellan's aura of a scholar and thick Scottish brogue added to the caricature. His white hair and unkempt eyebrows could have been his model for Nomos—or one of the staff of Hogwarts.

"Nice to meet you, Dr. McClellan...uh, Ben. I am not sure why I am here. I am a friend of Scooter's. I am also reading your book and enjoying it, but...like I said, I am not sure why I came." Harvey realized how he sounded a bit too serious. This wasn't an AA meeting...or maybe it was.

"Well, look, you didn't want to hear all that. It's nice to meet you, Ben."

After a few more minutes of greeting and chit-chat, Scooter called the gathering to order.

"Welcome, everyone. I am pleased so many of you could come. Does everyone have a drink and some snacks? Thanks to Bill and Samantha for bringing the desserts. Well played. There's coffee, decaf, and you can help yourself to anything at the bar."

He paused. "I wasn't sure I could pull this off on such short notice. Dr. McClellan, Ben, was available tonight and happy to speak to us. I think everyone has a copy of his little book, "*Tale of the Unlikely Prince?*" Scooter held one up for show. "How many of you have read it?"

Most of the women and many of the husbands raised their hands.

Scooter was gratified to see so many hands and graciously motioned to the others, saying, "Look, don't feel bad if you haven't read it yet. I am still glad you came. We can learn a lot about our quests tonight. Were you like me? I started reading—by the way—from my wife's copy of the book—without telling her." Several guests looked around and chuckled.

"I will say to you that I began my life hoping for a great quest, to prove to my parents, to God, and myself, I suppose, that I was a worthy son. I had a purpose here, not just some random struggle to survive or finish—but to do something great, substantive, and change the world."

"So, I can relate to that young boy's expectations—and maybe fears. Dr. McClellan, I mean that with all due respect. The book is quite simple—a short read—but I connected so quickly."

Many people around the room smiled and nodded, men and women alike.

"You too?" observed Scooter. "I can see heads nodding. What does it say about us? Or me? Just so no one is blindsided, I must say upfront that the book clearly has a religious and spiritual framework. It is not just an adolescent adventure fantasy. It has a deeper meaning. I will let Ben explain, but the *Tale of the Unlikely Prince* is partly about our longing to hear God the Father look down at each of us and say, 'Well done, good and faithful son or daughter.' Or 'this is my beloved son or daughter with whom I am well pleased.'"

"I am coming to see," Scooter said slowly and thoughtfully, "with some help from people like Ben, no matter what I am doing or have done in business, or relationships, or life, nothing scratches our deep primal itch—that longing in our gut to experience such a relationship right now, this very moment with our Heavenly Dad. Look, I'm 61 and just beginning to get this stuff. I have been a Christian for as long as I can remember. But I am realizing I have been a spiritual underachiever. I missed some very low-hanging fruit. I am still that insecure prince looking for affirmation from my dads and moms all around me. Does that make any sense? Sorry for getting so personal. You didn't come to hear from me." Scooter smiled, shook his head in self-deprecation, and chuckled.

"So, what I meant to say is welcome. Everybody, get your copies of *Tale of the Unlikely Prince* and prepare for some mind-blowing stuff. Tonight, we have the privilege of hearing from the author himself, Dr. McClellan, who will guide us through the profound insights of his book. Without any further ado, Dr. McClellan."

Dr. McClellan slowly stood up and lumbered to the front. He looked around like a short, chubby Cheshire cat—not creepy, charming with a broad, grandfatherly grin—infectious. It was apparent he was pleased to be here.

Ben began to speak to the group as if he were talking to a single close friend. There was a confidence about him and a wonderful spirit in how he spoke to the group, as well as an openness and an air of intimacy which someone later described as if they were hearing from a dear old friend they hadn't seen for a long time. Any concern or discomfort vanished.

"I am astounded," Ben continued in his mild Scottish brogue, "even shocked when real people truly get these concepts. I remember my Nana telling the bishop of our county back home, 'Yer bum's oot the windae!' You get the idea. Translated, 'You're not making any sense.' I think Jesus would cringe at how difficult we make His message. So, I usually start talks like this with a secular video that helps us better understand this good news. Scooter has graciously agreed to airplay this on his TV."

Scooter gave Ben the high sign that he was ready to roll. Everyone focused on the 70-inch screen behind Ben.

"Let me give you a bit of background first. I am concerned we followers of Jesus have misappropriated the good news—um, we misapply it. We make it way too heady and theological, dripping with insider language—so much so that I am not sure even we understand."

He warmly grinned. "We wrap ourselves with lists of moralistic expectations we attribute to God. Simply put, we foundationally believe if we do this or that—enough, whatever that means—or don't do something else, enough, that will determine what God thinks of us and whether He cares for us at all. Do you understand what I am saying?"

Most people nodded in agreement, including Pastor Rick. Harvey remained still, just drinking it in—both worried and expectant where this evening might be going.

Ben went on. "Yet, the core of the Gospel is so different, so much warmer and more personal. It's so simple we can miss its childlike wonder and mystery. So, I found this video helpful. It is called the 'Still face' experiment. It is troubling in some ways, especially for you who have children. But be patient. It has great imagery of what we are looking for from God. Scooter, please start the video. Can someone get the lights? It is only a few minutes long."

Scooter opened his laptop and pressed a couple of buttons. On the screen was a scientific researcher named Edward Tronick from Developmental Sciences at UMass in Boston—a distinctive, slight, grey-haired man, well-spoken. He looked a bit uncomfortable in a rarely worn brown tweed jacket, blue shirt, and paisley tie. He began his experiment with an infant and mother, explaining as we watched the interaction.

"Babies, this young, are extremely responsive to the emotions, reactivity, and the social interactions they get from the world around them. This is something we started studying…oh… thirty-four years ago when people didn't think infants could engage in social interactions. In the still face experiment, what the mother did is, she sits down and she's playing with her baby who is about a year of age. She gives a greeting to the baby and the baby gives a greeting back to her. This baby starts pointing at different places at the world, then the mother is trying to engage and play with her. They are working to coordinate their emotions and their intentions—what they want to do in the world. And that's what the baby is used to. Then we ask the mother to <u>not</u> respond to the baby."

It was a bit technical, but the video captured Harvey and the rest from the beginning. The mother and very young child were playing together, enjoying each other and being wonderfully normal. Then, at the scientist's instruction, the mother purposely changed her façade. She became emotionless and still faced. No matter what her child said or did, the mother did not react.

The child became frantic, acting anxious, worried, and even sad. She cried out, looked away and looked around for anyone in the room to connect with—until the mother, again instructed by the researcher, shifted back to being a loving parent. Almost immediately, the child followed suit and became happy again. The reconnection was initiated by the connecting and loving gaze of her mother's face.

Dr. Tronick concluded, not looking at the camera and somewhat awkwardly using his hands for emphasis. One imagines he is much more comfortable in the classroom or behind his glass window.

"It's a little like the good, the bad, and the ugly. The good is that normal stuff, that goes on, that we all do with our kids. The bad is when…something bad happens but the infant can overcome it, after all when you stopped the still face, the mother and the baby start to play again. The ugly is when you don't give the child any chance to get back to the good."

When the video stopped, Dr. McClellan stood and said, "Did everybody get what the child was going through? The mother, too, but let's focus on the child. All the child wanted to see in her mother's face was that she was special, worth the mother's time and energy. It was no doubt largely subconscious, deeply powerful. In the beginning, she could see her worth in her mother's face and her mother's eyes. She felt something external to herself that freed her, made her smile, laugh, play, and connect."

"When her mom's face went blank, the infant immediately changed. She couldn't help it. In her mother's vacant eyes, she lost her identity and value. She didn't feel noticed, appreciated, or loved. What kicked in subconsciously? She couldn't rest, play, smile, laugh, or be herself. She couldn't be creative. She became entirely stressed out: overwhelmed, anxious, troubled, frightened perhaps. She desperately had to find that gaze again, even looking around at the camera person—a total stranger for that gaze. She expends a lot of emotional energy to try to fix things."

"Then the mom's favorable and loving gaze returned. Did you notice how fast the infant returned to being joyful, loving, playful, and secure?"

He paused.

"This is us in our families, our relationships, our careers, our businesses, and our relationship with God. We are looking for that quality of acceptance in the gazes of others. When we don't get it, we become stressed out and anxious. Psychiatrists talk about our lack of ability to emotionally regulate."

"There is a lot of energy within us to find that benevolent and favorable gaze somewhere, anywhere: identities, sexuality, relationships, jobs, emotions. When we don't get it, there is a deep subconscious and nagging murmur of discontent and anxiousness.

Unaddressed, it changes us. Changes who we are. Changes the nature of our search for identity and relationships. Nothing is more important to us than whether or not we are in that immediate life-giving, or..." he paused for emphasis, "life-taking gaze."

"If we felt that life-giving gaze more often, we would be—like the baby—happier, more confident, playful, vulnerable, and creative—more you, more myself. We could love others at a far deeper level. On the other hand, deprived of that benevolent gaze from others and God, we will be very different. The difference is noticeable."

"One famous child psychologist, Urie Bronfenbrenner, put it this way, but it applies to adults too. 'Every child needs at least one adult who is irrationally crazy about him or her.' Me too, today, yesterday, tomorrow."

"My parents? My children? My spouse? My peers? How about God? If I really felt God's benevolent gaze today, on me right now, can you imagine, based upon what you just watched, how I would feel toward God in response? Or to others around me?"

Charlotte, Ray's wife, asked a question. "You said this is the Gospel. Can you expand on that a bit?"

"Yes, of course, dear lady," Ben paused, stroked his chin, and took time to consider his next comment. Harvey fully expected him to pull a long pipe out of his jacket like Nomos. He continued.

"So, remember back to your earliest understanding of what Jesus did for you and me. It is true what Jesus did on the Cross—His death for all of your—and my unfaithfulness against God, creation, and humanity—rescuing us from Hell (whatever that may be) and electing you and me to Heaven (whatever that may be) for all time."

"One old saint put it this way. Sin is looking for significance, security, and belonging anywhere other than in God's adoring arms, other measuring gazes—ye see."

"OK, that's great church-speak, utterly sound and orthodox. But let me put it in more of our language today, certainly the language of our young people."

"After what Jesus did for you and me, 2000 years ago, we have at least one person who is irrationally crazy about us. That can never change. We cannot mess it up. Believe me," he grinned, "I've tried."

"But after so many 'still face' disappointments, some from infancy, we all have a nasty, deeply entrenched critical inner voice telling us 24/7 it is all a lie. You aren't worthy enough that God would ever feel that way toward you. Oh, maybe he would love Mother Theresa, or Billy Graham, or Pastor Rick."

He pointed over to where Pastor Rick was sitting and grinned. The audience chuckled warmly.

"But not you, ye see?" he continued, walking around the front of the living room where the people sat in various chairs and sofas. The fireplace burned bright behind him.

"And the worst part about it is that inner dragon voice may not even be yours. Most often, it sounds a lot like your mother or father. How am I doing?"

The group was silent. Ben was doing fine.

"Yet in a more childlike place, when His Spirit found us, you and I were like that still face infant, desperately needing—far more than we were aware—a truly favorable gaze communicating to us that we were persons of great interest, worth, value, identity, and lovability. Look, nothing has hurt us more than relationships falling short of what we deserved, needed, and what we wanted.

This is a broken world, with so many broken people and broken relationships—none of which—no matter how good, truly fulfill our need for that measurement. Only God's gaze suffices. And it is very powerful. But to overstate our issues, on any given day, we are more like the distressed baby than we want to admit."

He paused to let the last statement settle. Harvey had never heard anything like this. Was it true?

"Before you were aware of what Christ did for you, Heaven felt still faced to you. Whether you know it or not, it is only human for your brain to feel at least some anxiety, fear, and sense of being abandoned, betrayed, lost, or orphaned. If so, then to one degree or another, everything you've done has been affected, good or not so good, every relationship, every choice, even your career path. Like the little one-year-old, your brain desperately, subconsciously, tried to replace that core gaze—and nothing worked. Oh, you may have had a good year, a profitable bottom line, performance awards, a huge tax return and felt momentarily good about your life. You emotionally regulated a bit. Very temporary. Very fleeting. Am I right?"

"You know, when speaking with my dear unbelieving friends, I like to graciously ask them, do you feel satisfied with your life, your success, your relationships, your purpose here? Are you ever truly at peace? Do you feel whole? Honestly, how's it going for you?"

Charlotte pushed back. "Ben, I have been a Christian for 30 years or so. I think what you are saying is spot on, but I am not sure how often I really get it."

"Yes," he quickly responded with a broad smile. "And so, *Tale of the Unlikely Prince*."

There was more nervous laughter from the group. Ben paused again to gather his next thoughts.

"Let me suggest it is a question of order. We all typically imagine if we are Christian, good, faithful, attend church, tithe, volunteer, give to the poor, don't drink too much—whatever your list may be—then God would necessarily smile over us. He would have to—kind of like a formula—or a celestial Coke machine. I put in the required coins and press a button, and the beverage of my choice drops out. Right?"

"Is everyone on board? So, in the context of the video, I just described the strategy of the distressed infant. She tried doing all the good things she could think of, hoping her mum would respond to her good works and love her back. She reached out to her mum (Prayer? Worship?)—hoping she would respond accordingly. But she didn't. The infant shrieked (Prayer, Worship, tithing, committee work, children's ministry)."

"Amen!" exclaimed an excited Pastor Rick, jokingly adding, "This is a good time to remind people there are still a few openings in the children's department."

Everyone laughed. The interruption gave people a bit of time to breathe and process all this new information.

"Aye," retorted Ben. "Like Nomos said to the prince, "Ye are a wee scunner, Pastor Rick." More laughter.

Scooter's wife took this moment as an excellent hostess to remind everyone of the goodies people brought. She invited the guests at the kitchen table to pass them around. More wine was poured. It was a good evening.

Dr. McClellan took a moment to eat a spicy deviled egg that Helene, Jim's wife, brought. "Old family recipe," she said. It was indeed superb. Dr. McClellan acknowledged her prowess with a slight nod in her direction. "Oh, this is lovely, my dear. I may get another one later."

Scooter stood to address the group as they took a much needed break. "I just read that the attention span of today's adolescents is less than a goldfish." People chuckled approvingly from around the room.

"But, at our age," he continued, "we have our own issues with attention. When I was 20, 'What am I doing here?' was an important existential question.

Now that I am 66, "What am I doing here?" involves staring at an open refrigerator."

"Let's reconvene in five."

19

T-Minus Five

"OK, OK, everyone settle down," urged Scooter gently, "or I might have to bring out another joke. Thank you for your time and attention; this is vital stuff. Ben, I know this is tough, but do you remember where you left off?

There was a pause as people returned to their seats, and Ben stood and rubbed his chin, which was a very Nomos-esque move.

"So, where was I? Hmmm, yes. We are like that distressed infant girl relationally and emotionally," he said, waving his short arms over the heads of the group. "We don't want to admit we jones for the positive measuring gazes of others that much. But we do! Science is proving it. The Gospel assumed it was true all along. The helpless child tried to regain her mom's favorable gaze—or even some counterfeit gaze, but nothing worked."

"We were left with a stressed-out child, acting out. If the experiment had continued—if the absence of the mother's favorable gaze was chronic, as is the case in many orphans or children whose parents were abusive or neglectful, the state of emotional stress may have become hardwired in the child's brain. Then the child would no longer expect such a favorable gaze from her mom, or anyone for that matter—no matter what she did."

"This was the unlikely prince. This is me. This is how many of us feel. We have been shrieking at God for so long and have cried out, begged, and slumped in our chairs that we risk becoming hardwired, and doubt God will ever like us, or maybe we imagine he has finally given up. 'Sure, God likes the good Christians, but something is wrong and foundationally unlovable about me.' We are like Prince Yeled, who couldn't seem to make any father proud. He messed up too much. God may like me in Heaven, but I shouldn't expect much now. What might prayer life or worship look like for such a person?"

Charlotte said, "Probably like my last week." Others chuckled with her. "Dr. McClellan, you said it was a problem with order?"

"Yes, thanks for getting me back on track. What if experiencing the benevolent gaze of the Father toward me comes first? That is one of the many stunning things Jesus purchased for me on the Cross 2000 years ago. Jesus' record of doing everything perfectly right is mysteriously put into my bio, and now God *must* love me. Of course, I am speaking from a human perspective—God must respond to me as if I had been a perfect son or daughter all my life. Or, in the *Unlikely Prince* terms, if I had been princely enough in my many quests. This 'righteousness of Christ,' for that is what the term implies, is already mine. God the Father *must* love me, and He adores me now as much as He adores the Son, and the Son adores the Father. He can't love me or you anymore or any less than that. We can't mess it up. No successful quest can add a thing to it."

"What would your prayer life or worship look like if you felt the love of Jesus for you right now? Imagine if it was an immediate response to His favor for you as you are—if you felt God adored you as you are. How would your time with Him be different if you could somehow mysteriously hear God say, 'Well done, good and faithful servant?'"

"Look, I am not trying to criticize anyone. My bent is to act like the still faced little girl."

"By the way, the technical term for the child who is confident of their mother's affection is 'secure.' Would you categorize our religious communities as primarily secure, or fearful, ashamed, guilt-ridden, anxious, and avoidant—in a word, insecure?"

"In *The Unlikely Prince*, Yeled is inherently insecure. The King's gaze has been available to him for years, but for some reason, he cannot experience it. He thinks a righteous quest will bring the King's gaze back, and it leads him down a dangerous journey—ironically, *away* from the King's favorable gaze. Tragically, he assumes the quest will do it. He fails miserably."

"Such is the nature and purpose of your quests and my quests. This is critical for us to see. Our quests, like Yeled's, are designed for us to fail. "All we need is need," one theologian once said, "but most of the time, we don't have that.""

"I don't want to spoil the book for those who haven't read it yet. But if you have read the first couple of chapters, you can see how the prince heroically tried to be a prince and do princely; why? So that his dads—both his new and old—would privately and publicly say, 'This is my beloved son, with whom I am well pleased.' He was that distressed infant shrieking. Yet, the King couldn't love the prince more than He did."

"And when the prince failed—and he failed big time—he could not imagine that returning to his father's gaze was a good idea. He didn't dare have such an audience with the King only to have still face—or worse in response. Irony again."

Harvey spoke up, surprising himself. "Like the still face experiment, the child was afraid her mother looked away because she was unlovable, broken, or ugly."

"Yes, exactly, subconsciously. It's brain science," grinned Dr. McClellan. "Harvey, you've got it. Why did Yeled need to prove to the Others he was not a loser? In a neuroscientific sense, he had to—I do it all the time. But it was beneath a true prince."

Harvey realized he hadn't finished the book. "What happens to Yeled?" he asked himself as he looked at the book in his lap.

"Other questions, anyone?"

"You are saying God already likes me, as I am—and even though my brain is beat up and distressed as much as you say, I can experience it more now?" said Scooter.

"Yes, of course," Dr. McClellan enthusiastically nodded. "Jesus paid dearly for that. It is yours already. Faith is all that is required. May I read a Bible verse for you? This is from Paul's letter to the church in Ephesus, chapter three, and we will begin with verse 14. By the way, trouble was in store for the church in Ephesus. It was in a tough city, largely antagonistic to the Gospel. They were on a quest that they would fail. Paul doesn't pray they would get more money, or building, or success—or even more volunteers for the children's ministry," Ben quipped, looking over at Pastor Rick. "All of those are good things. Somehow, Paul understood that they—and we today, need one thing. See if you can hear the one thing he repeats." Here is what Paul says.

"For this reason, I kneel before the Father, from whom his whole family in heaven and on earth derives its name. I pray that out of his glorious riches he may strengthen you with power through his Spirit in your inner being, so that Christ may dwell in your hearts through faith. And I pray that you, being rooted and established in love, may have power, together with all the saints, to grasp how wide and long and high and deep is the love of Christ, and to know this love that surpasses knowledge — that you may be filled to the measure of all the fullness of God."

"Did anyone pick up the repeated theme?"

A couple of people blurted out, "Power."

"Yes, exactly. It happens to be two different Greek words, but the meaning is similar. So, let me ask. Have you ever been told that as a child of God, you *must* ask God for His power—through the Holy Spirit in your inner-being—before you can even begin to grasp the love that Christ has for you and others around you? Only through that heavenly-sourced power can you feel God's love for you—all due to Jesus. Look, this is not academic. This is real-life stuff."

"Did you see how it changed everything about the little child? She became 'her' again. That's bad grammar, but you know what I mean. So, it must change you and me as well. The transformation should be observable—it must be. All you need to do is ask. Let me be clear and personalize this. If I don't access Spirit-sourced power from God first, I will not be able to experience the love of Christ for me today. I will be spiritually still faced."

"That love is there. Jesus paid for it. It is all around us, but we so rarely feel it. It's a brain thing. I can't just strain and choose to feel God's love. I need to access power first. Has anyone told you that? Doesn't it explain so much about our Christian walk? We are often boring and insecure princes and princesses loved by the great King, but we imagine if we pulled off some great quest, we would finally feel the King's love. Balderdash. We are all 'wee scunners.'"

"But what if we ask and nothing happens?" said Harvey.

"Yes, exactly. Harvey, right?" Harvey was impressed Ben remembered his name. "May I observe something, though it may offend you a bit, my new friend? That statement is birthed, no doubt, from the still face exercise going on too long for you or me. You are not alone. All of us have been affected by faulty, imperfect relationships since infancy—all of us. And so, we are riddled with ongoing subconscious fears and doubts, wondering if we have messed up too much or failed our fathers or mothers—all causing us to doubt God likes us. It's part of being human in this cold, selfish world. This is where God finds us. This is where the King found Yeled. Harvey, this is all of us."

Harvey didn't know what to say or if he should say anything. He just turned his eyes to the book and shook his head slowly. "Was he right?" he wondered to himself.

"All of us carry so many relational scars. We are not able to count the still face moments in our lives, some by close family, friends, broken marriages, absent parents, and parents who themselves had suffered from so many still face episodes they had no idea how to make us feel favored. It wasn't in their tool chest. It is an epidemic in this fallen world. Paul calls it 'groaning.' Then we Jesus-followers project these still faces onto our relationship with God. My father, who passed away years ago, was extremely moralistic and could be quite critical. On Sunday, we *had* to go to church, sit quietly, repent of our weekly crimes. Then, we would go home to do nothing that God could possibly construe as sinful. What does a six-year-old make of that? Don't get me wrong. My dad was a good, very well-meaning, but hard man. His father was even harder."

"I will tell you I still hear his voice when I make foolish decisions. I see his gaze of disappointment, judgment, and even anger. I am still hardwired to expect the same treatment from my heavenly Father."

"Yes, good news. This is where God found us. This is where God finds us tonight and tomorrow. Most of us had such good and well-meaning parents. Some of us did not. We are all in the same boat. We all have hardwired doubts, fears, shame, and perhaps even guilt. Some more than others, but it is universal. So much so it would take a miracle for me to look up by faith to God's eyes and expect to see Him laughing in pride over me, bragging about me to the heavenly court, 'Hey, look at my beloved son, Ben, my pride and joy.'"

"So now what? It may seem like our situation is pretty dire. Not so. Here's the easy part. Stop what you are doing and ask God to make it happen. Ask over and over for God to give you His 'faith,' and by that, I mean what one theologian called the 'secret workings of the Holy Spirit in you,' the power that comes from God and has the stuff to override your doubts and hardwired fears of failure."

"I am not sure I get it," Harvey said cautiously. He was not comfortable being this vulnerable, but at this moment, he wanted answers more than he feared the risks of exposure.

"It is difficult to change and even harder to admit the need for change. As a successful businessman, you might find it exhausting."

Harvey chuckled under his breath. "If you only knew," he thought.

"I am inviting each of us to accept that our fears of being rejected by God, of looking up to see a blank face are real and bigger than we have imagined to date. We are in a worse place than we know—me too. You probably can ask your spouse—they might just tell you how needy you are."

The women nodded.

"So, admit it to God. 'God, I am ashamed, more than I realize. God, I am afraid that I have messed up. I feel broken somehow. God, I know I haven't been faithful enough. God, if I were you, I wouldn't like me. God, I am tired of trying and getting nothing but still face from You."

"Then preach the Gospel to yourself. Here, take a look at these bookmarks. Pair off and say this aloud to each other—first one, then the other. I wanted to make this very practical and easy tonight. Dragons can be very slippery, you know by now."

"It's not a prayer, per se—more of a gospel presentation to my nasty, critical inner dragon. In terms that Dr. Tronik would appreciate, I am leaning into that hardwired inner working model in my midbrain that keeps me from feeling the excitement in my mother's gaze."

Scooter had a handful of colorful bookmarks he handed out to everyone in the room.

Harvey paired off with the hostess, Scooter's wife, Marge. The small bookmark print required his reading glasses, so he reached into his jacket pocket and put them on. Motioning to Marge to go first, he listened and read along.

"Jesus-Follower, strictly because of what Jesus did for you 2000 years ago, Jesus loves you with all His heart, as much as the Father loves the Son and the Son loves the Father. God loves you as you are, not as you should be or could be. You can't add to this love or take away from it. It often feels like you've messed it up or need to do something so God will like you better. Not so. How do you experience it more? Simple! Ask the Spirit inside of you to make you know, experience, and feel just how much God loves you right now. Just ask. Ask again later today. Ask tomorrow. Make it a spiritual habit."

When she finished, she looked up into Harvey's face. Her eyes were moist with tears. He was embarrassed by her vulnerability. So, he quickly looked down to his card resting in his large hand and followed suit.

Once everyone had taken a turn, Dr. McClellan got their attention again.

"Well now, that wasn't so painful. Here's the audience participation portion of the evening. Would someone like to begin by telling me what struck you in the prayer? What grabbed you? What jumped off the bookmark? What bothered you? What did you disagree with? Every comment is kosher here. Go for it. Hmmmm. Who would like to go first? Harvey looked down to avoid Dr. McClellan's gaze.

Marge raised her hand and shared, "I guess I knew this already, but it felt strange to hear I can't add to God's love for me. I get it in my head, but I am uncomfortable living out of that. I don't have any other template for that kind of love. Do you know what I mean?"

Next came Harold. "But if this is true, isn't this enabling bad behavior? Isn't guilt a corrective of bad behavior? If I told everyone God will love you no matter what, what is to stop a person from going crazy and doing all kinds of bad stuff—drugs, porn, affairs—you know?"

Dr. McClellan nodded thoughtfully and smiled. "Yes, yes, good question. Ah, but it seems to me that guilt hasn't been very successful, has it? My gran once tol' me, if you guilt a guilty person, you just end up with an angry guilty person. Their heid's mince (Their head's a bit mixed up), ya see? Even the Apostle Paul emphasizes in his letter to the Romans that it is God's kindness that leads to repentance. Surely, if guilt were effective, wouldn't he have mentioned it? Perhaps, he was on to something, eh?"

"I find that telling sinners about the God that loves the unlovable, the unloved, and the unlovely doesn't enable sin at all. The change may not be noticeable all at once. Mony a mickle maks a muckle! (Investing a little bit at a time soon becomes a large amount). And ah dinnae ken (I don't know), but it seems their sinning's already enabled—and it isn't scratching their itch very well. Maybe it's time to try something different. Eh?"

One of his bushy eyebrows rose on his forehead, and he grinned like an old Chesire cat. "Someone else?"

A few more people shared. Harvey was growing increasingly uncomfortable. He had something to share but was way past his vulnerability quotient.

Then, as if someone had come and thrown him a face-saving rescue, Harvey's phone rang. He had forgotten to mute it—embarrassing, for sure. He urgently got up and went into the other room before he pulled the phone from his jacket to look at who was calling. It was Sadie.

"What's up?"

"Harvey, we need to talk."

He looked at his watch. "I'm driving by the plant to get home anyway. I'll see you in 10 minutes."

Harvey made his apologies and goodbyes and left in a hurry. He got to the plant in less than ten minutes.

Sadie was on the phone again. He pointed over to his office. She understood the corporate sign language. She held up five fingers—five minutes. Harvey knew she probably meant ten.

He went to his office and sat down. It was late and he didn't want to start a new project, but he had something important to ask Sadie.

He pulled the small book from his satchel and thought he could squeeze in another chapter or two from *Tale of the Unlikely Prince*.

20

A Little Past Ouch

The storyteller went on:

"Prince, Prince..." Yeled heard the voice again—a much kinder voice. It started off very quiet, as if it were from a great distance, but then grew louder.

"Prince, Prince, wake up; it is time to move on now."

When the prince awoke, he was back in bed—this time, sadly, a regular run-of-the-mill straw one. "Too bad," he thought. His head was still pounding, and though his wounds were dressed, his whole body ached horribly. His face was drenched with tears. So much had happened in a very short time.

The Royal Steward was shaking him, trying the best she could to wake him from his sleep. She was very concerned, of course. She had placed an immense number of smelly herbs, aromatic gooey salves and bandages on the prince's bites, cuts, scratches, whelps, abrasions, lacerations, gouges, scuffs, matted hair and, of course, many multicolored bruises. He winced at the fierce stink in the room and wondered if they were near a sewer. But soon, he realized the stink was him.

"Where am I?" His voice cracked. He was surprised to see he was still wearing his mangled, now blood-stained surcoat—or what was left of it—over what was left of his torn-up linen tunic.

"What happened?" he wondered to himself. His eyes shot around the room, looking for any clues. He even tried to get out of bed but was still too woozy to move. He could only sink back under the plain, rough wool comforter with a loud moan. His pillow, he noted, was far from superior.

Then the memories of recent days and events began seeping back into his recollection. There was the embarrassing confrontation with the Others, and then the horrific nightmare. But most of all, he remembered the incident with Dolos and the Royal Steward. Before he could say anything about it, the Royal Steward spoke.

"Welcome back to the land of the living, my prince, the beloved of the great King, the King's son."

"Where am I?" asked Yeled. "The last thing I remember was being in the castle of Lord Dolos—weeks there, in fact—and about to become his son. But then he changed... He wasn't kind at all. He was a..."

"Deceiver?" interrupted the Steward, nodding her head. "A snake? A liar? Yes, unfortunately, he was very real. I am sorry to say, not a dream—not like we think of dreams. Rather, maybe it is best to imagine him and his dark world as part of an alternate reality, where time and substance are out-of-sync with our reality—though still very destructive. In truth, you have been in this very bed for two days. I was very worried about you."

"Days!" exclaimed Yeled. "What do you mean? I was with Dolos for weeks."

"My prince, I have not left your side. I assure you. Your episode with the Others was only two days ago. It is confusing, but trust me, all will be revealed to those who are the King's."

The prince tried to get up but still felt a stabbing pain in his side.

"Please rest, my prince. You have bruised your ribs, maybe even fractured a few."

"Ah yes," Yeled nodded assent as he lay back on the hard pillow. "The beating from the Others. I suppose I messed up badly?"

"Yes, pretty much," said the steward, immediately nodding her assent, not in a judgmental way at all. "You didn't really stand a chance. Though you were quite valiant. After it was over, I flagged down a passing cart, and we got you to a nearby village and to this inn. You had a high fever for the first eight hours. I wondered if we would lose you. I was able to find local herbs and medicines at the market. I think you will be fine. Sorry for the smell, but you must take some time to heal."

"Time?" He asked, feeling some urgency now. He tried to get out of bed once more—will he never learn? Princes and princesses most often lack patience. I have researched it widely.

Though he tried, he only felt light-headed and had to lay back on his very unsatisfying straw pillow. "I had this crazy dream, a nightmare. My father was there; it was horrible, and when I saw his face, it wasn't his; it was mine. I don't understand. And then there was the Dolos thing. And you were there. You just rolled up the whole world as casually as someone would roll up a dusty rug. What... Who are you?"

The steward discerned it was time to explain some things to the prince. It was his quest, after all. He should begin to understand.

"Well, to start with, I too am concerned about your nightmare. There are deep-seated issues within you slowly robbing you of joy and hope. Trust is a very difficult thing for you. These issues are very powerful and so must be resolved by an even greater power. This too shall come to pass, more than you are aware.

"But Dolos? What is he all about?" said the prince, cutting her off as he frustratingly waved his arms in the air, suffering a stab of pain in his side for his troubles and his lack of patience.

"My prince," said the steward with great compassion. "I am sure I have said to you not all quests are the same. And truly, not all quests are what they seem."

That hardly helped. Yeled was even more confused but realized he needed to clear the air a bit.

"I have many questions but want to apologize to you, Steward. I have never even asked you your name. In fact, I don't know much about you at all. But what you did for me back there in the dark valley, and what you did to Dolos... It was...well... Who are you?"

The steward took a moment to gather her thoughts. She had known this conversation would eventually come. It was time.

"My name is Noomai. I have been with this King since the beginning of his reign. I proceeded from him with the charge to proclaim his character and nature to his people. I speak to any and all about his innate love for the unlovable, the unlovely, and the unloved."

"And to unlikely princes who fail their quests?" Yeled said with a nod.

"Especially them," Noomai said, smiling a most beautiful and endearing smile.

"So, Noomai, may I call you that?" She nodded kindly. "Who or what is Dolos?"

"It is a good question, my prince," said Noomai. "You know more than most who he is and what he is capable of. For a time, a little time, the serpent is allowed to roam the world and is made to be useful in the great King's larger, invisible plan. At some level, Dolos may even be aware he has limited freedom and even less time. He can go no further than he is allowed.

Such a vast irony. He is not only a powerful liar—in fact, there is none greater—yet he cannot even begin to see how crippled he is by his own disgusting lies. I assure you, he has no chance of defeating this King or his purposes, and since I go forth with the power of the King, he has no power over me either."

"So, are you saying he serves at the King's pleasure too?" asked Yeled with eyebrows furrowed.

"Yes, in a sense. He would never say so, of course. Yet all the kingdom serves this great King, whether they are aware of it or not, including snakes.

It comes back to the role of quests. All our journeys are made up of one quest after another. Each is ordained by the King for good. As you are beginning to see, no quest, including yours, is ever what it seems to be at the beginning. This King, your father, is without a doubt not what he appears."

"My quest?" asked Yeled, pausing. "Do I still have a quest?"

"Of course, my prince. But your quest," Noomai said, complete with air quotes, "will just have to wait a while. You are now officially on a quest-sabbatical."

Obviously, the last bit about the quest-sabbatical was totally made up, but it calmed the prince down some. It sounded legit to him.

"Oh, what difference does it make anyway?" The prince said, self-pity rising. "I have totally messed it up, haven't I? In the history of quests, this must be one of the worst." He looked away from the steward in shame.

Noomai smiled and said, "Yep, easily top five." She chuckled. When he realized she was joking, he smiled a little too. It really hurt. Then he chuckled, which hurt even more. Which made both laugh even more—which, well, you get the idea. They started giggling, chuckling, and laughing out loud with even a chortle or two, and each time the prince winced in pain, it started the whole guffawing thing over again.

The prince finally begged, "Oh, please, stop; don't make me laugh again. It hurts too much."

A couple of minutes of more-or-less silence passed.

"What am I going to do now?" he opined. "I only know how to be a prince—and a poor one at that. Am I to return to the Kingdom and face my father? Face his official disappointment and shame. Face the mocking from the people? From Nomos?"

"My prince," Noomai began with as much compassion and caring as anyone could muster. Gone was the frightening, larger-than-life façade Noomai had manifested in the presence of Dolos.

Now, she was humbly dressed in a comfortable white tunic. The prince guessed she had burned her gooed-up garment. She had also taken the blue ribbon from her hair, allowing her flowing white curls to drape softly over her thin, dark shoulders. Yeled noticed how attractive she was. He wondered what it would have been like if his mother were like her. Would he have turned out differently?

"My prince, no such thing will happen," she continued. "I will say to you once more, your father, the King, loves you with all the love in the Kingdom. He cannot love you any more or any less than he did before the quest. You cannot mess up such a love. I am certain of it."

"I want to thank you for your support and words of kindness, and for what you did to save me from Dolos—and myself, I suppose." The prince tried hard to say the right words to the steward, but he held no silly notion he would ever be welcomed back by this King—much less held in honor by him. The King was a great king and deserved a great son. He was just not that son. He had proven it.

But the steward is right about one thing. He must go and face the music, his last pathetic act as a prince.

After a few more days of rest and recovery, the two weary travelers hit the road again—this time on the long journey back to the castle. The prince was still embarrassingly dressed in what was left of his shredded surcoat on top of a thin linen tunic. He looked more like a beggar than a prince.

Noomai had done the best she could to clean up the coat of arms from the spider goo and sew up the surcoat where it was more or less respectable—at least at a distance.

But spider goo is nigh impossible to clean off. In fact, one industrious person was making bank marketing it as Flex Spider Goo. "Now you can fix your broken mead cup, mend your broken jewelry box, or even repair cracked arrows. Check it out; one drop of Flex Spider Goo can lift five dragons at once." The marketing was indeed impressive.

But I digress again. My bad. So much to say and so little time. The point is the prince still didn't look like a prince, and he surely didn't feel like one.

As they silently trudged step after step toward the Kingdom and, of course, the King, Yeled did what depressed people often do. He did a mental inventory of his life. His mind went all the way back to his childhood, long before the uprising in Garden City. Life was good then, he remembered, but he was just a child. Those times seemed good. Future bright. Everyone looked up to his mom and dad.

Dolos had lied about that. Maybe they were a bit demanding. Or something else. Hmmm.

Then, things went badly. There was the coup and the poorly thought-out cavalry charge (he was willing to admit that now). There was the hurtful thing his dad said to him before the charge. "Boy, make your mother and me proud of you this time."

On their own, perhaps the last words were forgettable, but considering the following events, Yeled just kept repeating "this time" in his mind. "You mean there were other times?" His eyes furrowed together in some dismay as he thought about the significance. It sat in his head like a rotten piece of meat would sit in a stomach and make it turn over and over.

Did you know there is part of your brain where all your "ouches!" register? It's true. Whether you get bit by a spider, step on a rock, feel lonely, or if someone says something hurtful, there is a part of your brain designed to say, "Ouch!" Yeled's brain was saying 'ouch!' a lot, as much for the memory of the last words his father said as for the many owies he had suffered on the quest. And, he thought, his brain was also saying 'ouch!' for all the things his father didn't say, like "I am so proud of you, son!" You know.

He looked down at the dusty path in sadness. He wondered if he could only see his birth father again, would he ask what he meant? But alas, what a foolish thought. It can never happen. All he ever wanted to do was make his father proud of him. No judgment from me. All of us want to do the same thing.

Boys and girls, I will let you in on a little secret. Until that particular virulent "ouch!" was dealt with, Yeled still couldn't accept kind words from anyone, including the King. Even when the King said he was proud, Yeled couldn't process it. It's not all his fault. Dolos was not all wrong.

THE LAST QUEST

And here's the thing, and you, being a smart audience member, likely already figured this out. Quests are not designed to heal such wounds. They don't have the power. This is where this particular special quest is spot on, and most other quest stories fall very short.

How many quest stories have you heard where the prince or princess goes out, fails to slay a dragon or two, falls into depression, wants to quit—but then solves the mysterious riddle of their coat of arms? It's an 'aha!' moment in the quest tale changing the royal's entire worldview. Using the secret of the coat of arms, he or she becomes a giant dragon slayer. Right? Then the moral of the typical quest tale is this: If you, like the prince, finally get the secret of the coat of arms riddle and can choose to incorporate it into your life, you too will become a great prince and live happily ever after—if you only do it enough.

Well, such things are just pulp fiction—run-of-the-mill quest tales, to be sure. Do you know what I mean?

We want to believe the knight would finally be successful, rise over their suffering if only they could figure out the secret of knighthood (the coat of arms), and boom, the "ouch!" would at last be healed.

Nope! Won't happen. Oh, don't get me wrong, it feels good to be regaled by a large audience for your accomplishments, to go on the vast quest-speaker circuit, to write "how to succeed in your quest" books—you know. But unresolved hurts will remain. They are deeply rooted and very powerful. It is even harder when, like Yeled and maybe you, there is no way to talk to the person who hurt you again. I am getting way ahead of myself, but there is one mysterious place where such a healing of secrets can take place. Ah, I have said too much for now.

Oh, I should also mention, we haven't said much about the coat of arms, have we? I promise you more is to come. It does hold mysteries, for sure—just not what you might expect.

"Oh, why did I push for this stupid quest?" said Yeled, berating himself one more time. It was easy for Yeled to criticize himself. Now, he must face the music.

The quest had, for all practical purposes, been grounded to an ignominious halt. They were limping home in disgrace. He had hoped there would be songs written about his victories and glory. Now he could only imagine the silly embarrassing songs written about him and this quest. Forever, he would be the unlikely prince.

Noomai knew better than to say much more at this point. She would have a moment soon. They had lost their rides, both horse and donkey, their supplies and their weapons. She purchased some dragon jerky and skins of water tiding them over, as long as they didn't run into any more dragons, spiders or gnomes. Or Others.

So, what do you do when you feel like it's time to give up?

A knight on his quest meets a wise teacher on the road as he is traveling. The man asks the teacher, "Which way to success?" The robed, bearded sage doesn't say anything. He just points into the distance. The knight is thrilled by the prospect of finally experiencing success in his quest and runs off in the appointed direction. Suddenly, there comes a loud "Ouch!"

The knight limps back, a bit tattered, assuming he must have misinterpreted the message—and taken the wrong road.

He repeats his question, "Which way do I go to be successful?" Again, the counselor silently points the knight in the very same direction. The knight shakes his head but obediently walks down the path once again. Maybe he did something wrong? Maybe he needed to have his sword out? Maybe the path is clear this time? It doesn't take long; once he is out of sight of the counselor, the air is filled with an even louder cry, "OUCH!" along with a deafening, crushing sound and a spew of fire climbing the horizon.

When the bloody and charred knight crawls back to the feet of the sage, he angrily complains, "Twice, I asked you which is the way to success?" He swallowed hard and took a needed breath. "I did what you said, but I was crushed by the dragon of defeat twice. This time, tell me the truth, old man."

Unmoved, the wise teacher compassionately looked down at the pathetic glory-seeking knight, and quietly said, "Success is that way. Just a little past 'Ouch!'"

21

BO

Harvey's reading of the *Unlikely Prince* was rudely interrupted by a surprise phone call. His whole body jerked. The caller ID said it was his son, Bo. "Oh, my goodness. It isn't Christmas yet. He never calls any other time." He quickly answered, hoping beyond hope that Bo was alright.

"Bo, is that you?" Harvey blurted out, his heart rate racing. "Are you OK? Is anything wrong? I should have called, but this has been a bad couple of months for me, very bad..."

"Dad, Dad, stop. I'm OK. Really. It's good to hear your voice. I am sorry to hear that you have been struggling. Me too, I suppose. There's something that I need to talk to you about. Is this a good time?"

Interesting question, Harvey asked himself. This was anything but a good time. But it was Bo. "Of course, buddy. This is a great time. I may have a meeting in a bit, but that can wait. How's Melanie and the boys?"

"Oh, fine, fine, I think." He paused. "Hey, Dad, listen, I took a leave from the firm. Well, to tell you the truth, I *had* to take some time—what we are calling a 'mutually agreed upon sabbatical.' I needed to get my act together, not just for me but for my family too. Uh, you see, Dad, I'm not sure how to tell you. I am an alcoholic, well, and a drug addict too. I could control it for a while, but it got out of hand recently, well, for a year or so."

Harvey was trying to remember how old Bo was, maybe mid-40s. Bo was struggling to hold back tears. Harvey could tell. "Melanie took the kids and is with her sister—she has been for a little while now. It's my fault. We are getting counseling; it seems to be helping, I think. I am also going to AA meetings every other day. I am sorry I haven't told you, but I was worried you would be disappointed in me."

"Oh no, kid, you are not a disappointment. You are amazing. I should be telling you that more often." "Well," he thought, "I guess I should have told you even once."

"Thanks Dad. All that said, I am going through the Steps now, and I am talking with people that I have harmed. You are on my list. Are you familiar with the 12 Steps? 'Step 8: Make a list of all persons we have harmed and be willing to make amends to them all.'"

"Bo, you don't need to make amends with me. I probably need to make amends with you."

"Dad, stop; I need to do this. It is my path to healing. Listen, when I left, I was angry. I'm still not sure what I was angry about. I have always seen you as one of my heroes. What you have done and accomplished in your career is amazing and enviable. My counselor says that maybe I felt threatened by your success. I don't know; it sounds so selfish to me. My AA mentor says it was all about justifying my addiction. I was doing coke at the time. It doesn't matter why I did what I did to you. I just cut you out of my life, left you in a lurch—no explanation. Apparently, I do that to Melanie, too. I am still trying to figure it out, but it seems to be a pattern."

"Oh, Bo. I am so sorry."

"Look, Dad, there is no reason for you to be sorry. I see now that I meant to hurt you—and probably did. Please forgive me. I will figure it out. But for now, please accept my confession as it is. Maybe more to come down the road. I want to have you back in my life. I am pretty much on my own out here, and it sucks, I tell ya."

He laughed, and Harvey chuckled, too. Harvey wasn't sure what to think or feel. Was there a hurt in his heart from Bo's departure? Now that he thought about it, it was surprising and hurtful. But it was just business, he had said to himself then. Now, he's not sure what that even means.

"Of course, son, I forgive you. I am here for you anytime. After this chat, I think...I think that you are my hero."

"Thanks, Dad, that is so good to hear. You give me hope that I am not a total screw-up. I will tell you that I have been sober for six months now. My sponsor says that I should be very encouraged. Melanie and I met for lunch the other day. It was pretty awkward, but there was some promise. She is very hurt—well, to be honest, I have hurt her badly. I don't know if she will ever forgive me—or should. My oldest is in her third year at the university. Not sure if she's wants anything to do with me either. Well, one day at a time. Oh, listen to me. I haven't even asked how you are doing. You mentioned that you are going through a tough time?"

"Oh, not to worry, Bo. You know me; I will pull a rabbit out of my hat sooner or later."

"Yeah, I expect no less from you. Hey, Dad, do you remember when James and I were just kids, and you were trying to get us to bed?"

"Yeah," said Harvey, suddenly being flooded with memories—good memories."

Well, most of the time, you would tell us off-the-wall fairy tales about some kingdom filled with wonderful assembly lines and high-profit widgets, being attacked by nasty greedy trolls called Fifth Third Bank, magical flying pigs from the IRS, and ugly dragons from the horrible kingdom of OSHA?"

Harvey had to chuckle. "Yeah, my bad."

"No, they were great. You said they were the same stories your father told you and your brother. James and I figured you were making it all up on the fly. We didn't care. We were having a great time. If you wanted us to get to sleep, it was a terrible strategy."

"Yeah, that's 'bout right," Harvey agreed. "I was tempted to give you kids some antihistamine to knock you out. But looking back, they are good memories."

"Hey, the reason I bring it up is I remember one thing you said to us. I don't remember the story, but I remember what you said just before you turned the light out one evening. You said, "Not all quests are the same." You probably don't remember, but I do. That little phrase has helped me more than you know. No matter how many bad things have happened in my checkered, turbulent life, I remember that I am not alone; I am on a quest—a quest specially designed for me by the Great King—uh—that's a topic for another day.

You know, I was reminded of it last week when my AA sponsor said the same thing to me. I just had to laugh. So, I wanted to thank you, Dad. You have made a real difference in my life. I mean that. I love you."

"Hey Bo, you have made my day—no my week–with this call. But I need to go. Can I call you this weekend? I want to hear more. I miss you so much, and I am so proud of you."

"Yeah, Dad, uh...why not? Anytime would be fine. I've got nothing to do except meetings. Love to catch up, I mean really catch up."

"Me too. Goodbye for now," Harvey responded as he hung up.

He didn't really have to go. He was about to break down in tears, and he didn't want Bo to hear him that way. Old habits are hard to break. He took a couple of deep breaths, trying to fend it off, and rubbed his reddening eyes. But the flood of tears came.

After a short while, Harvey sat at the desk and grabbed some more tissues.

"Is my family cursed? Have we done something horribly wrong, and the ruler of the heavens got his nose bent out of shape and is smiting us." Harvey remembered an old Gary Larson cartoon with a boy walking right underneath a grand piano that was being lowered down to the sidewalk by a crane from a second-floor window. In the next frame, God sits in Heaven with his finger above a 'Smite' button.

That's how Harvey feels—his dad, his brother, his own business, and now, Bo.

"God, what have I done? Tell me, please, I'm begging you. Please tell me before it's too late."

It's strange where the human brain goes. Harvey thought about the video he had seen of the little girl at Scooter's house when she realized that her mother didn't care for her anymore. What was it called? That's right, Harvey remembered. She felt still faced—no explanation, no provocation—yet everything good in her life was ripped away. And there was nothing she could do but shriek.

But then something else was bubbling up in Harvey's gut, diametrically opposed to what he was feeling. Bo called him his hero. "I sure didn't expect that. Maybe he's right. Maybe this is just another of life's many quests?"

Or was it? Harvey realized he was firmly holding the *Unlikely Prince* in his grasp.

"OK, fine, God, please show me something." He opened the small book to chapter fourteen, "Wee Scunner," and read some more.

22

YE WEE SCUNNER

The storyteller went on:

After they climbed a short rise, they could finally see the great King's castle, a long day's journey still.

The prince's emotions were roiling in his gut. Sure, he was relieved to be back, but he knew the next few days would be very painful for him.

"Castle Gazette Headline! 'The Unlikely Prince Comes Home After His Ugly Failed Quest,'" Yeled imagined in his head. "But at least he salvaged his coat of arms—or at least bits and pieces of it!" he smirked as he looked down at the once-colorful crest, now just a carrier of hardened spider goo. The prince was depressed.

"Haud yer wheesht!" came a familiar voice from a patch of trees immediately off the road they were traveling. (That is Scottish for 'Just hold your tongue and listen!') It was Nomos. "Fit's 'at aboot?" (What's all that about?)

"Boy!" exclaimed the height-challenged Nomos as he lumbered toward the two travelers, his leather sandals slapping at each step. "I have bin lingering in this glade fur a long while to find out if the rumors are true. And listen, a nod's as guid as a wink tae a blind horse." (Meaning: explain yourself and make your meaning clear.)

Yeled couldn't help but smile at his former mentor. He had forgotten some of the Scottish-isms, but he was so glad to be in safe company again.

"Well," Yeled began, with a broad smirk on his face, "to be sure, it's a dreich day!" Typically, this Scottish phrase refers to a miserable, cold, wet day in reference to the weather, but Yeled meant it more broadly. It referred to his very bad quest.

Then Nomos laughed out loud and warmly hugged Yeled for a long time. Nomos kissed the tearful Yeled on both cheeks.

"Aye, I missed you, you wee scunner!" exclaimed Nomos as he wiped a tear away from his bluish-grey eyes with his rough woolen shirt. (In Scottish, it means 'you little problem child.' Nomos meant it endearingly.)

Nomos' eyebrows were still full of shocks of white hair defying gravity and logic. Once, someone suggested he trim them. Nomos said he would miss such old and trusted friends.

"Tell me, lad, 'ow's the quest? Did you slay that nasty dragon?" Nomos asked, bringing up the elephant in the room.

"Nomos, with all due respect," opined Yeled. "I have failed badly. I have brought disgrace to myself and shame to my King. I am not worthy to be called his son."

Nomos paused for a while, not saying anything but compassionately gazing into the young lad's eyes. Then he spoke. "Oh, you foolish lad. Yer bum's oot the windae!" (Meaning: you're not making any sense.)

"You don't understand," Yeled said as subconscious defense mechanisms began to swell within him. "I failed the quest. I wrestled with many dragons, but…"

"Ah, lad, dinnae ya hear me. I didn't ask about those dragons. I could care less about those insignificant reptiles. I asked if you slayed the dragon. That was your quest, you see." Nomos paused and rubbed his full beard thoughtfully. What he said next was very unexpected.

"Laddie, may I have your permission to tell ye about yer mother and father?"

"My ma…my pa?" said a clearly confused Yeled. "Did you know them? I mean, were you in Garden City?"

"Aye, I knew them well," said Nomos. "None were closer, except the king, perhaps. Long before you came along, to be sure. There was a time…" Nomos said, almost drifting off, deep in thought. Tears formed in his eyes. He cleared his throat, wiped the tears away with his rough woolen overcoat, took a deep breath, and began again.

"Aye, there was a time when the two of them were something very special. None were more caring and compassionate. Your parents would do anything for anyone, especially the King. It was said they were the embodiment of the first two elements of your coat of arms, mishpat and tzedakah. They always put others first and then made things right if people were treated unjustly. They were filled with the spirit of the King like none before or after."

"But then, mysteriously, they turned; each inexplicably reached out and grabbed darkness instead of light. Some say, and I agree, they were tricked, but once the deed was done, they changed. They turned inward and self-focused—like frightened orphans who, at the end of the day, were desperately dependent on their own efforts and wiles to survive—no longer trusted anyone, especially the King."

"Wait," said Yeled. "Are you saying... wait, where was the King when all of this happened? Why didn't he step in?"

"Ah, no, it was they who abandoned the King. The King never abandoned them—not this King. They hid, not the other way around."

"And so, sadly, when ye came along," Nomos said, nodding his head and raising his bushy eyebrows for emphasis, "they had so little to give you. It's not all their fault, you see. You needed to see in their faces you were the most special child ever. You needed to hear again and again how wonderful you were and it didn't matter if you did this or that well, or well enough.

They couldn't give ya what you needed. They had lost it themselves. They were empty cups desperately trying to be filled any which way—well, except the one. But they were too proud, too ashamed or maybe too afraid—just too human—to look up into the adoring and forgiving gaze of the King again. They spent the rest of their tragic lives hidden away in Garden City."

"So," asked the prince in a rare moment of great clarity. "Are you saying I could never make my father proud of me? Not really?"

"Aye, that's the tragedy of it for you. Ya dinnae have that kind of power. Even the Royal Steward here can't do that. Yer ma and pa needed the King, but... there it is. Empty cups just can't fill other cups."

"Oh, my prince, to the point," said the Royal Steward with such spirit-empowered compassion. "What Nomos also means to say is quests can't heal those deep inner wounds. They are not designed to."

"Aye, ye scunner, ya see, yer quest isn't done yet—not near," said Nomos as he winked at the Royal Steward as if they shared a secret.

It turns out they did.

Nomos asked again, "Boy, tell me about your success with slaying the dragon."

Yeled was caught off guard. "Master Nomos, I would rather not go down that path again. It was, uh, a disaster. I could not have done worse."

"Balderdash!" exclaimed Nomos as he threw his stubby arms into the air. He spoke so loudly a flock of guineas erupted from a nearby ridge of grass.

"Boy, you dinnae hear the question right again. Will you tell me about your dragon? Those other beasties come and go. I'm talking aboot the real dragon."

The Royal Steward saw this as her cue and invited the confused Yeled to sit down on a nearby log. She put her arm on Yeled's left shoulder and slowly patted as if in rhythm with his heartbeat, calming him down and opening his mind to receive the truly good news he had never been able to hear before.

"My prince," the steward gently added, "you are, whether you know it or not, even though you never asked for it; you <u>are</u> a child of your father and mother. Inside your head is a hungry dragon voraciously consuming almost every compliment, every statement of love and every so-be'd honor. The beast quickly extinguishes any feelings of you being enough. Your dragon has been there for as long as you can remember and beyond, preventing you from feeling like the son any father would be proud of. So, the rest of your brain just kept working on feeding your beast. It's not all your fault. And so, your quest was ultimately designed for you to face that dragon—your dragon."

"I don't understand," exclaimed Yeled. "How can I slay a dragon I can't see? How can I slay a dragon that is in me? Is me?"

"Ya can't," said Nomos, interrupting as he placed one of his stubby fingers along the side of his nose to suggest, at last, the great secret was out. Nomos took out his long pipe. He had long given up smoking. It's bad for your health, you know. But it calmed him to put the unlit pipe in his mouth.

Then Nomos continued his thought. "That's the whole point—the irony of it all. Ya can't. You did all you could do, and it wasn't enough to even prick that dragon in ye. Now you have two paths left. You can keep feeding your inner dragon for the rest of your life. Good luck with that. You will never feel good enough. You will never feel your father is proud of you—enough."

"Or you can finally admit you can't do it and run helplessly to the arms of the King. There's real healing power there and there alone. Do what your parents wouldn't do—couldn't do. The choice is yours, lad."

The prince didn't know what to say. This was not what he was expecting. Is it true? If so, he'd lived his entire life chasing a lie or, worse yet, unknowingly trying to feed a hidden dragon whose hunger was unquenchable. Were they right?

"There's one more thing, my great prince," added the Royal Steward. "It's all been in your coat of arms."

You see, I told you we would get back to the coat of arms. Just not the way you were expecting. You'll be surprised, I think. Oh, back to the Royal Steward.

"My prince," said the steward, "at the very top is the victory of the King over that dragon, the very same one who tricked your parents. All else, lipnay melek, mishpat and tzedakah, are in the shadow of that great victory—you could say sourced by that lone victory."

"Now go to the very bottom. Lipnay melek. There is no path to becoming a great prince or princess where you don't run and throw yourself into the loving arms of the King over and over again. You must first be loved, honored and adored, and there is only one place where such a thing truly occurs. Isn't that what you've been longing for so long? Your parents were too proud or too afraid to submit to the King's great forgiveness and love. Until you experience lipnay melek, you have no power to really do mishpat or tzedakah anyway. You are too needy yourself to have anything to offer others."

"Empty cups can't be mishpat or tzedakah. Oh, they can try. They can go on quest after quest, but it is the lipnay melek of the King alone which can make one love others over oneself, even if it costs dearly. Your parents were lipnay melek until they weren't."

She went on. "So how do you gain this powerful healing spirit, the lipnay melek? To state the obvious, it is only accessed in the presence of the King, face to face, gaze to gaze, eye to eye, lipnay melek."

"Empty cups will begin to be filled only as they hold empty hands upward in his arms. 'Father, I can't do this. Fill my cup and still my inner dragon a little or a lot today.' Truly great princes do this daily, for the dragon is never truly gone, only defeated daily by an even greater power."

"The key to experiencing what you have longed for all your life is not out here slaying this or that dragon or trying to prove yourself to Others. Do you want to feel truly good enough? Enoughness only happens lipnay melek."

Instinctively, she wrapped her arms around his shoulders and hugged him close. "You are so loved, my prince. Far more than you can grasp at this moment. More than your inner dragon will let you, but you have never been closer to it. Breathe. Hear this, the voice of your King. 'You are my beloved son, with whom I am well pleased.'"

Nomos also had more to say. In fact, he was just warming up. He had waited a long time for this. Hardly fair.

"Prince, hear me well. It is lesser princes who look for honor in all the wrong places and end up settling for so much less or nothing at all. They end up children of their parents, tragic empty cups."

"So, if I was so unprepared, then why was I sent on this quest?" The prince complained unprincely.

"Remember my prince? Ye requested it from the King. It was yer idea all along."

"The wink—of course!" thought the prince to himself.

"Irony again, ya left the presence of the King to find a putrid substitute for the presence of the King. But the further you went away, the worse ya felt. Simply put, the King knew ye would fail, humanly speaking. It was the goal of the quest, or at least the first level of the quest. Sometimes such shaming is a positive thing. In fact, redemptive shaming is a very good thing—or so I hear." He said the last part with a wink, a grin and a high jump where he clicked his heels.

"Even failure in the careful hands of a wise King can lead to an end far greater than all the successes of all time rolled into a single humongous ball. If, in yer failure, ye would come to see that ye are in greater need than ye have ever before imagined, it's all good. All ye ever needed was need, and ye dinnae have that until noo. And if the failure brings ya into his arms, what say ya?"

Nomos gave Yeled a toothy grin. He had practiced that line, and his delivery was flawless.

"Teacher, I am undone," Yeled uttered in a very reserved tone. "I sit here now, terrified to look into the eyes of the King, afraid of the reflection I will see. I couldn't stand rejection. I couldn't."

"Aye, remember, all ye need is need! Do ye have at least that? We will see. You can't avoid it. Your King and Father await your return."

Yeled shuddered noticeably. He wasn't sure about all he had just heard. He needed time to process, but he knew he needed to end this quest, no matter what.

23

SADIE'S QUEST

At last, Sadie knocked on Harvey's open door. "Good time? It took longer than I thought." She was amazing. She brought him his usual cup of java from the Starbucks just two doors down—grande dark roast with ample cream and two Splendas—extra hot. This was comfort food for Harvey.

Sadie's crystal blue eyes—still young, he thought—looked out over her reading glasses. "Yeah, come on in," Harvey quipped.

Sadie entered Harv's office and stood in front of the desk. Quite formal, Harvey thought.

She looked at the ground and hesitantly began, "I was going to see you earlier today, but things came up."

She sounded foreboding. "Wait, Sadie, me first." Harvey was surprised at the sense of urgency in his voice. "You have known me for a while. We have been through a lot together. Apart from Eleanor, you probably know me as well as anyone. Hey, you probably know me better than my wife."

He chuckled; however, it was probably true. Harvey and Sadie were never romantically involved, far from it. Yet Harvey didn't open up to too many people—working ten hours a day alongside Sadie for so many years made for some familiarity.

"Harv, what's up? You seem troubled. Just spill it."

"Am I over the hill?" Harvey blurted out. "Done? Is this it?"

"Where is this coming from?"

"We lost the Barr account."

"Yeah, I heard from Sebastian. That will hurt the company significantly. We certainly didn't need bad news right now, did we? I need to sit down. May I?"

"Sit, of course." Harvey's eyes scrunched together and pointed to the chair in front of his desk. He came around his desk and sat awkwardly on the sofa perpendicular to her. She was worried before about the business and her boss and friend—now she was *very* worried. This is just not like him. She leaned back to steel herself for what might come.

"Look, Sadie, I am feeling…a bit beat up. Not just the economy or the business—that too. I am feeling washed out…old, you know? I don't think I can do it anymore." Harvey was not looking at Sadie as he spoke. He gazed out the window far into the distance. If there was ever a picture of melancholy, this was it.

Sadie wasn't prepared for this. She needed a strong, confident, leader, Harvey, right now. The company required warrior Harvey right now, not the crumpled, defeated, self-focused, disheartened, tired old man slumped on the sofa before her.

"Have you spoken to Eleanor? I mean about this. Does she know how you feel?"

"What…uh no. She couldn't handle it. She needs me to be strong right now…for her. Her sister is dying. I think she suspects trouble at work. She doesn't want to know. That's the game. When she has a problem, I fix it. When I have a problem, I fix it. I'm not sure I can fix this one."

"Oh, Harvey. I am so sorry."

"Look, Sadie, I don't want your pity. Please tell me you still believe I will pull a rabbit out of my hat again. I need you to have confidence in me again. I need to see it in your eyes. You know my dad was never around. I think I had to step up and be a man too early. My mom was never a provider. So, I filled the gap. Sometimes, I want to hear my dad say, 'Good job, son. I am so proud of the man you have grown to be.' Do you know?"

Sadie could only listen quietly to this despondent man in front of her. In some ways, he was so strong, and in others, so needy. What could she say? It was difficult to see a way out of this one. She wanted to be honest—that's what friends do, right?

"Harvey, I am so sorry. I don't think there is ever a good time for this conversation, but maybe now is as good as any. Maybe we should shut it all down. Liquidate. Sell the equipment to other companies and ride off into the sunset." She glanced down for effect at the crumpled financial papers on her lap.

"There is no shame in what we tried to accomplish. Many have done well here. You have quite a legacy, even if it doesn't end as we had hoped." She was trying not to tear up.

"Look, I have been running some numbers. I think we can break even if we act quickly. Value Corporation has contacted me to explore our interest in selling out. They might even be willing to keep many folks on. I thought you needed to hear that from me before the staff meeting tomorrow. We need to get back to them by the end of the day."

This was not what Harvey wanted to hear. Not at all what he needed. He curtly thanked Sadie for her honesty—but didn't mean it. "I have to think about it. Go home now. The rest can wait until morning, can't it?"

She looked down at the ground. It was too painful to look at Harvey's face. "I'll just leave the email on your desk. Good night, Harvey. I am so sorry."

"She doesn't believe in me either," he thought as he drove home. He had never felt so alone, so isolated—even in those early months after his dad's funeral. Though a teenager, he had intentionally decided to be that provider for his mom and later his family. He believed in his ability and knew others could see it, too. He felt successful. That was then; this is now. Now, he felt inconsequential and irrelevant—a bust.

He just needed to get home before his emotions took over. He needed to breathe. He was so glad Eleanor wasn't there; he wouldn't know what to say—or how to say it.

When he got home, he got into his bedclothes and reclined into his spot on the sofa. He needed to chill and settle his thoughts. He glanced over at the book.

At that moment, right there on the forest-green, overstuffed couch, he had an amazing epiphany. He finally realized he was that distressed infant in the video. All around him were still faces. Ben was right; it was worse than Harvey thought.

What was wrong with him? He had heard him talk about the favor of God. It couldn't have been clearer only an hour ago. Then he went and ignored God again. What must God think now? "If I could look up now, I don't expect He would be pleased with me...again."

24

The Coffee Shop

Harvey stumbled into the Hub, the university's kitschy equivalent to Starbucks. It was raining cats and dogs outside. Unfortunately, the only umbrella Harvey had in his car was his massive Titlist golfing umbrella. It was the size of a small country, eye-popping yellow, and very wet. He had to do that awkward thing with the umbrella—close it without slinging too much rain on other people. There was no easy way to close it and still look sophisticated. We have all been there, done that.

In contrast to the outside, the Hub was dry and pleasantly warm, largely due to a raging fire in a wide nook to his left. Multiple students had gathered around it with their cappuccinos and grande lattes. "They just keep getting younger," Harvey thought.

Harvey would not linger. He had a mission, a quest to be sure. He glanced around the room to find the person he had come to see.

"Woo hoo, Harvey, is that you?" said Ben, a bit too loud, and waved his hands at him a little too enthusiastically for Harvey's comfort. "It is a pleasure to see you again and so soon. Please sit down. May I get you some hot cider, tea, or whatever the young people drink here?"

Harvey noticed Dr. McClellan looked directly into his eyes as he spoke. It was not offensive; rather, quite endearing—in fact, quite grandfatherly.

He was surprised Dr. Ben McClellan had agreed to meet with him today. He said on the phone that he was pleased that someone had read his tiny book—much less had questions—he was such a kind and humble man. Then, in a heavy Scottish accent, he remarked, "My dear ol' Nana used to say, 'Guid gear comes in sma' bulk,' meaning 'Good things can come in small packages.'"

"Dr. McClellan, uh look, I should be getting *you* coffee…I am in your debt, uh…I…"

"Please call me Ben. Do you see that young girl behind the counter? That's my granddaughter. Just tell me what you want. Please sit down and join me at my table. We can talk freely here, I assure you." He had found a table at the far back of the Hub, four wooden chairs around a large keg with a tabletop.

"Uh…Ben…OK, coffee, whatever is dark today, cream, and two Splendas—would be great. Thanks."

"Sabrina dear…woo-hoo. Dear?"

The attractive young girl sprinted around the counter to attend to her grandfather's pleasure.

"Sabrina, this is Harvey, my new friend. He would like a large—or whatever you call them here, dark coffee with cream and some delicious fake sugar. Did I hear correctly? Please be a dear and put it on my tab." He winked at her.

"Yes, thank you, miss," Harvey said to the attractive young co-ed. "Uh, two Splendas would be great." Awkward. She traipsed off behind the counter—delighted to wait on her grandfather.

"Oh, dear, you are soaked to the bone. It's a bit of a dreich day," Dr. McClellan said with his Scottish lilt. "Would you prefer to be by the fire?"

At that moment, Harvey noticed that Dr. McClellan really did look like an overstuffed garden gnome. It made him smile.

"Uh, no...thanks," said Harvey awkwardly. "I'm fine. So, like I said on the phone, Dr.... uh...Ben, I am reading your book, *Tale of the Unlikely Prince*. I...uh...have some questions. Do you mind if I ask you something? It is a bit embarrassing."

"Let me guess, dear boy, you have found yourself on a quest as well—or more to the point, you have failed your quest? Eh?" As he said it, Ben's face lit up with an elfish grin—once again, not offensive or arrogant, yet knowing.

"Yeah, that's about it, I suppose. Pretty obvious?" Harvey shook his head and looked down at the tabletop. He was a bit embarrassed, but at least he didn't have to say it aloud. "Do you get this often from people?"

"Oh yes, you'd be surprised how many failed princes and princesses are out there. I am one, too. The book is an autobiography of sorts."

Sabrina walked over with Harvey's steaming coffee in a large stone mug and set it down in front of him, carefully laying the two Splenda packages to the side.

"Thank you, dear girl," said Ben broadly, smiling at his granddaughter. She was obviously very appreciative of her grandfather's words. Then Ben brought his full attention back to Harvey. "So now, where were we? Aye, yer failed quest. Please tell me about yourself, Harvey. You seemed very troubled on the phone."

Harvey spent the next fifteen minutes telling Ben as much as he could about the business and the recent downturn or as much as he thought was appropriate for a non-business academic. He assumed most professors don't particularly care for bottom lines, staffing, income statements, budgets, and marketing—probably found it all very dull. He shared about his father's unfortunate death and told him about his conversation with Sadie last night. All the while, Harvey was quite worried about what the professor would say. It did not appear he was surprised, not at all—or bored. He was a remarkable listener. At no time did Harvey feel judged or patronized.

Time passed, and Harvey realized he had totally monopolized the conversation. Ben had not yet said a single word since Harvey began speaking. He just kept looking deeply into Harvey's eyes and periodically nodding to express he was following, or so Harvey assumed.

"Dr. McClellan," Harvey blurted out. "I am so rude. I have been talking this whole time, and I haven't let you say a single thing."

"Nae bother. Yer na' rude. But certainly, I have rarely met a more needy person." Dr. McClellan smiled disarmingly again. It was a joke, or at least Harvey thought it was. "How can I help you?"

"I'm 69. I have been around the block. I've had business successes—many, in fact. I have a few good friends. I have a faithful wife, my second wife, who has stuck by me. And yet, I feel broken somehow, like I am missing something."

At that moment, there was an extended silence in the coffee shop, as if everyone collectively took a break from the chit-chat. At least, that's how it felt to Harvey. It made him feel very exposed.

The professor leaned forward, looking straight into Harvey's eyes, and grumbled a crude sentence; surprising for this character, Harvey thought to himself. It was barely loud enough for Harvey to hear yet designed specifically for him.

"There is a saying among the Scots, '*It's a sair ficht for half a loaf.*'"

"What?"

"Roughly means, 'Life is hard work. It's a sore fight, and ya only get half of what ya want.' To be clear, shame's a real schmuck. Eh?"

"Excuse me?"

"Well, to be precise, shame is a real schmuck-maker."

"I'm sorry?" Harvey was taken aback.

"Yes, of course...uh...May I? I do not want to be indelicate, but may I tell you about your father?"

"I'm not sure what you mean?"

"Aye, of course not. Again, not to be impertinent, but may I play the role of Nomos from the book for a bit? May I tell ya about yer Da'?"

Harvey was speechless.

"Yer da' was a good man, yet he couldn't give ya what ya longed for." Dr. McClellan spoke compassionately and endearingly without an ounce of judgment or shaming. "'E loved his boy dearly. Of course, the boy loved his da's attention. In the end, the da' could not be what the child needed. Good work ethic, no doubt. A provider. Aye. However, the child was left feeling alone and isolated missing something that only a good da' can provide. The poor boy was stuck in his own 'still face' experiment. Of course, I am referring to the video I showed last night."

Harvey leaned back in his chair as if clubbed by a blunt instrument.

"Your ma? If I may...Hmmm," Dr. McClellan continued with a broad grin.

Harvey couldn't believe his ears. This conversation had taken a strange twist.

"Yer mum was a good lady, a good mum to be sure; however, she could do little to unravel the growing cocoon that increasingly encompassed the boy—you. Aye," he nodded slightly.

"Perhaps she had a cocoon as well, to some degree, a cocoon partly of her own making, no doubt. She was on her own bonnie quest, to be sure. Ah, but this was of little value to a boy who dearly wanted to be loved and appreciated by his da, who wanted his da to tell him he was so proud. And so, yer life quest, my boy. Do you see it now?"

"See what…I am not sure what you want me to see. My father died when I was a teenager. He *was* a good man. I have many memories of laughing together, playing football, and making model planes. Sadly, the worst happened. So, of course, I left school and became the head of the family. I had to provide. My mother couldn't deal with it."

"Aye, of course, my new friend. I am sure you did it bravely. You would have made yer da' very proud. That has been your quest all along. It has been to please yer human father. Answer this question. How has that gone for ya?"

Dr. McClellan paused for effect. Harvey said nothing.

"You see that all-too-normal young man was left with a hole deep down in his young, thirsty soul that needed to be filled. There was no one else to do it. His da' was no longer there for him. It was his journey alone, which he took on without complaint and has never stopped. You are that infant in the video, needing that gaze but not seeing it."

"And so here you are. You want your da' to be proud of you. You long to see—as all children should—the deep love and respect from your da's eyes. You want to hear your father say—as all children do—'Well done, my son, with whom I am well pleased.'"

"Now, ye are sensing ya are near the end of yer human quest, and the prince has failed, ya' see? It was an impossible quest to start with. At what he assumed was the end of the quest, when he should finally hear 'Well done, faithful Son!' nothing is said, only silence. He didn't achieve his goal. The truth is he couldn't. The decks were stacked against him. That was, in essence, the whole point of the quest."

"And all too naturally, shame rushed in. That is shame's nature. It's how our heavenly da' made it. Tragic questions. 'What did I do wrong?' 'Could I have done something differently?' 'Have I made a mess of things?' 'What might my da' think of me now?' 'What would a better son have done?'"

"Then shame, using its despicable and vile split-tongue, whispered to the lad speaking in first person. 'Maybe I am not a real prince.' 'Maybe I am not a good provider.' 'Maybe I am not as good a businessman as I thought?' 'Maybe I am not worthy of my da's love.' 'I am just a false prince, a step-child, a failure. No wonder my da' left.' 'All this sacrifice and I leave the world empty-handed?'"

"How am I doing?" Dr. McClellan asked the dumbfounded Harvey.

"Now, if those voices are left unchallenged, the quest for that young boy ends—and ends badly. The quest dissolves and the boy must settle for...well, who knows what. Or he may self-medicate the pain; no great coat of arms, no real glory, no legacy, and certainly no sense of the love and favor of his Heavenly Da, the only gaze that truly gives life. Your business cannot do it, Harvey. Your relationships cannot. Whether you are known as a genius by your peers or not. Only one gaze can rescue."

"And so now what?" Harvey interrupted the elderly truth-teller. "Now what?" he said with an inner silent groan.

Wisely, Dr. McClellan said nothing.

Harvey's impatience finally got the better of him, and he erupted. "Let's skip all the psychological claptrap. Sir, please get to the bottom line. Are you saying I'm done? That I *have* failed? I screwed the pooch. Perhaps my dad left me an emotional basket case? My first wife suggested I keep seeing our counselor. Perhaps if I had, all would be different?" He sighed deeply, pausing as if trying to grab hold of something elusive in his brain.

"Ben, can I ask you a question? If my father *were* here, do you think he would be disappointed in me?"

"Dear boy, dear boy. Hear me. Look me in the eyes. I don't suspect that's true at all. That's certainly shame talking. That is the voice of an insecure child. Yet, from what you've told me, you are a good and faithful son. If your human da' were here, I have no doubt he would agree without hesitation. Maybe now, he would have the ability to hug you, to tell you how proud of you he had been. Wouldn't it be so wonderful for that little boy who has always down deep, wondered."

Harvey was fighting between frustration and depression, a very unfamiliar space for him. "Somehow that doesn't make me feel better, Ben. I still feel like a failure!"

"Yes, of course you do. That makes all the sense in the world. Don't ya' see?"

"I am lost," Harv waved his hand slightly, dismissively perhaps, and turned his eyes away. "Look, you just said if my father were here, he would tell me I was a good son?"

"Yes, of course. That would perhaps be good, suitable, and sufficient for a *regular* boy." Dr. McClellan clearly emphasized the word *regular*."

"However, ye are not a regular boy. Ye are a great prince. Ye have been given not just a quest, indeed a *great* quest—a quest only due a *great* prince. As good and as normal as your desire is to hear your da' praise you, your heart demands even more. It can only be satisfied by the adoration and praise from a *great* King. That is your real quest."

"The fear is you might settle for lesser adoration, lesser gazes. Tragic indeed. Praise from peers, success in business, awards, comfortable houses, and hobbies. Or the absence of all of the above. These things, no matter how wonderful and good they may be, will never quench the thirst for the life-giving favor that great princes long for."

"This is the nature of a great prince's desire—and it is a good desire, natural to great princes, far beyond what human parents can give—alive or dead. The lie is that your da'—no matter how kind and gracious he could have been, should have been, or might have been—even if he had not taken his life—he could not have quenched such a great thirst of such a great prince."

"You are speaking of God again, right?" Harvey responded as he leaned forward a tad.

"Aye, of course, dear boy," Dr. McClellan said with a chuckle as he sat back. "There is no greater King. You deeply thirst to hear, 'My Prince, well done, good and faithful servant.' That will be satisfied at no other throne."

"This is such good news, Harvey. Your quest has been long and arduous. Yet, it is far from over. If your quest were over, then perhaps you would be a great and tragic failure of epic proportion."

"My new friend don't listen to yer inner dragon. It is yer shame that would make ye a functional schmuck, a stepchild of little innate honor or name. That is a lie. Oh no! Yer quest is far from over. Ye must now choose to continue yer search for life-giving favor in the gaze of yer heavenly Father who loves ye more than love itself. *Lipnay Elohim*, literally 'in the presence of God,' in front of God's face, up into His Holy grill, eye to eye, your gaze to His. His Son has already irrevocably earned it for ya'. So, ya' cannot make him more proud or more pleased. Or ya' can find other gazes. Yer choice. But how's that goin' for ya'? What will ya' do, son?"

"I canna' give ya' business advice. Scooter seems pretty capable if ya' need some advice on the nuts and bolts of sound financial decisions. I am just preaching the gospel to ya', reminding ya' what ya' already know. Whether yer business succeeds or fails, God loves ya' the same. Ya' canna' add any honor to yer name than being adopted as a son of the Living God. The only thing that can ever make ya' satisfied is the ongoing favorable gaze of yer King. Look up, prince, look up. It is a problem of order. Run and jump into the arms of God and feel his pleasure for you, as you are first. Business is always second. Ya' will notice a difference. Others will too."

"Ya' said ya' haven't quite finished my little book? May I request something from ya'? May I personally read the last chapter to ya'? I think that will make some sense. What do you say? Are we on?"

That was out of left field for Harvey, for sure. He didn't see that coming. Dr. McClellan was willing to read his book to him. Here? How strange. It took him back to the wonderful times when his dad read him books in the old living room before bedtime. He loved those times. He misses them.

"Well, boy, I don't want to intrude into yer time, but I think it would be a good use of our time together. What do ya' have a mind to do?"

"Yes, if you are willing, I would enjoy that, "said Harvey. "I was surprised someone like you would do that for me. Just saying."

"Aye, but it is a true honor fer me to read to a great prince as yerself. May I have yer book, please? I just didn't bring one with me. May I?"

"Of course," Harvey said, still shocked at where this morning was going. He handed Dr. McClellan his copy of the *Unlikely Prince*," actually Eleanor's copy, and sat back. He took another gulp of coffee but found it very tepid. Strange how coffee only tastes good either hot or cold, he thought. Dr. McClellan turned to the last chapter and cleared his throat. Harvey listened with great interest, hoping to find a clue of what to do now. What was it he really wanted?

25

Finale: The Great King

T he storyteller went on:

As the three travelers began to approach the royal city, a loud trumpet blew, ripping through the clear blue skies and interrupting the slight breeze. It was so loud it could be heard throughout the vast kingdom.

An armed entourage, mounted on great fiery steeds, exited the massive golden gates of the castle at full gallop. There were seventy-seven men and seventy-seven women—great warriors and heroes all. Each wore grand bronze helmets fitted with red plumes. Each carried body-length shields proudly portraying the great coat of arms. Each was fitted with fine, craftsman-made swords strapped to their waists.

Their splendor made Yeled feel so small and unimpressive. His shredded surcoat looked even more ragged and baggy, as if his shoulders weren't wide enough to fill it.

The royal troop headed straight for the three exposed travelers. Yeled searched his mind for a word to describe the regal cavalcade. He landed on two—impressive and frightening.

In moments, the soldiers completely surrounded them. No matter which way you turned, there were tall horses standing in your way. They were snorting and swishing their long tails, scraping the dust with their hooves.

For your information, when horses are happy, they tend to snort. Not so for humans. That would be very awkward and off-putting. Not knowing much about horses, Yeled was feeling very exposed and threatened. Don't fret. I am not done with my tale. Okay, where was I? Oh yes, horses snorting, swishing, and scraping.

After a long pause, the western portion of the circle—the part closest to the castle gate—intentionally opened. Bright rays from the setting sun poured over Yeled, Nomos, and the Royal Steward. A new shadow appeared virtually blocking out the sun. It was the great King entering the circle. He was riding a pure black stallion so massive it made all others appear like mere ponies.

This was indeed a very great King.

"Prince..." roared the King, his voice echoing with seriousness and gravitas in the hollow formed by the circle of skilled warriors. His expression appeared quite solemn, even angry toward Yeled. His black eyebrows knit together severely. This is exactly what Yeled was afraid of—but also what he expected and knew he deserved.

"Prince," the King began again with a very grave and demanding tone. "How was your quest? Did you complete your charge? If I recall, you were told—by me..." The King put his finger to his lips and looked upwards as if saying this from memory.

"Thus, it was said, 'Every...EVERY aspect of the quest WILL be accomplished. There can be NO failure. You WILL find what you are looking for. No veering to the right or left, no hesitancy, no disappointment, for any negligence or dereliction at all would be quite consequential to you.'"

"Do you recall?" The King interrogated Yeled in a very off-putting loud voice. "This was the quest YOU requested—no more and no less. So, tell us about your travails. Tell us of your great, memorable battles—the great victories. Tell us about the honor you have earned. I wait. No, we wait." The King waved his arms around the armed soldiers. "Speak!"

The prince felt his pulse skyrocket, his legs felt wobbly and he worried he might throw up the jerky beginning to twist and turn in his warm stomach. He shrugged his shoulders and took a few shallow breaths. Then some more.

What could he say? He had no heroic tale—very few victories to speak of. This was going to be worse than he imagined. After a very long moment, during which the prince mainly looked at the ground, he began.

"Uh, great and mighty King...uh... Father...I...I didn't..."

"STOP!" yelled the Great King, cutting him off. Fierce royal eyes burned toward the hapless Yeled, and he quivered in trepidation. He had never heard the King so angry, so firm, so intense. This was quickly going downhill. At this moment, he had forgotten everything Nomos and the Royal Steward had told him.

The King shook his head in obvious disgust, his lips pursed and his expression dire. He swept his gaze across the circle of men and women, loyal warriors all. All eyes were upon the King, waiting for what he would say and do next.

Yeled was filled with apprehension and shame. Who wouldn't be? No judgment from me.

"Look, my faithful and trusted warriors," the King said as he pointed their attention to the nervous young man. "Behold my son, Yeled." He paused and even shook his head in disgust. This was indeed Yeled's worst nightmare.

Then the strangest thing happened. The King's face broke out into a huge royal smile. Then he laughed the greatest, deepest and most unexpected royal laugh ever laughed by any royalty anywhere before or since.

I have researched this thoroughly. There was a laugh by King Richard of Kent a decade or so ago when the Queen bore him triplets. Then there was the guffaw of the great Queen Simone after her army, made up entirely of women, had defeated another army made up of only men. As laughable as those laughs were, they were nowhere near—on the universal laughability scale—as laughter-rating as this King's laugh.

All his troops joined him, including Nomos and the Royal Steward. Everyone, except Yeled, was bent over in laughter. Only Yeled didn't get the joke, not yet anyway.

"BEHOLD!" the King proclaimed with a smile of great joy on his face as he pointed toward his confused and embarrassed son.

"See, my son, my beloved son, with whom I am well pleased and love more than love itself—he has returned from his holy quest. He has come into my presence, lipnay melek at last. I have missed him so much."

The Great King dismounted from his great steed and approached the prince with open arms. "Come into my arms, my son. Look up into my eyes and see how much I adore you as you are, not as you think you should be. I know what a great prince you will become. I am confident of it. But first, receive MY spirit, MY mishpat, and

MY tzedakah. Your inner dragon is great, but it is no match for MY love."

The prince didn't wait until the King had finished his sentence. He threw himself into his kingly arms and wept. Never had he felt so welcomed, so honored, so valued. This...this is what he had been longing for—for so long.

After a few moments, the King raised his eyebrows and turned his head, feigning being critical. "What happened to the sword I gave you? And are those bee stings? I thought you hated bees. And what is that smell?" he grimaced a kingly grimace. "Spider goo?"

There was a wave of chuckling from the group—not critical at all. It was a chuckle from peers—a respectful chuckle. That is a very different thing. The King smiled openly and authentically at his bewildered son.

"Everyone, gaze upon him," the King proclaimed. "He is Sir Yeled, the rightful heir to the throne."

At this, the riders each dismounted, and to a person bowed to the ground in honor of the new knight of the realm, Sir Yeled.

Yeled couldn't breathe. This was not at all what he expected. He was struggling to make any sense of what just happened. One thing is for sure: this time, he felt something different.

After they all bowed, the soldiers circled Yeled, patted him on the back, and congratulated him on his new honor. This was a great thing; this was the highest level of recognition offered by the realm—apart from adoption, that is.

What happened, you ask? Well, if you've been listening to the tale, you should know the nature of this King and his love by now. The King's love for his son cannot be stronger; it cannot be diminished. It didn't need a quest, successful or not, to be proven or earned.

In Yeled's defense, how could he have known about such love before his adoption? He hadn't received anything close from his biological father or mother, to be sure. Only this Great King's love is, by nature, so loving.

"My beloved son, Prince Yeled," said the King with a voice so warm and endearing, sounding more like the Royal Steward than Nomos. "Welcome home. My castle is just not the same without you. Now you know the mysteries of my love. My love is for the unlovable, the unlovely, the unloved, the undesired, and the undesirable. It is even for those who, like so many, feel like disappointments to their fathers and mothers. I love failed princes and princesses. That's all there is."

"And failed stewards," said the Royal Steward a bit sheepishly, though with a smile.

"And failed viziers as well," winked Nomos with a Scottish dance of some sort.

"Look around you," added the King. "See the dozen-dozen warriors who now embrace you? Like you, some of them were also orphaned; some were addicts, homeless, riddled with unforgiveness or just angry at the world. Some were rebels and bullies themselves; others hated me and what I stood for. That's where I found them."

"The same dragon in their brains had devoured any sense of worth, honor or being desired or desirable. Each first needed healing through my love and my embrace. Some were even more stubborn than you. Is that even possible? There is only one power greater than such a dragon. The experience of my love in my presence *lipnay melek*, is the only power able to even begin to slay their own inner dragon."

"Now you see the goal of your quest wasn't for you to succeed or earn my love. You really must hear some of the hilarious stories from these other men and women who went on their own quests with very similar outcomes.

A couple of them had to fight flocks of relentless, crazed chickens. Others had to deal with endless computer spam messages that some total stranger in a faraway country across the ocean had left his entire estate of $1,232,500 to you as long as you sent them your Social Security Number. Very tricky, indeed. No one had done well when confronted with Others."

"They each failed miserably too." The King paused and grinned. "Not as badly as you, my son. To be sure, you have set a new bar." The group of soldiers all shared a laugh. Yeled chuckled too. He was not offended; in fact, he felt only respect from his peers. His dragon had been stilled for now.

"No," the King continued with a joyful heart. "The purpose of the quest was for you to begin to see your problem wasn't what has or hasn't happened to you in your life, your successes or failures, the amount of love showered upon you or not by your parents. It was solely designed to expose a hidden internal enemy preventing you from feeling any honor or love. You already had my love but couldn't receive it. You are not alone."

"All I need is need..." Yeled remembered being told repeatedly by both Nomos and the Royal Steward.

"Be wary," said the King. "Your dragon is only <u>mostly</u> slain, my son. It will rise again and again. You will learn to regularly access my powerful love in my presence. I will make it so."

"Now, having said that," the King chuckled. "Still, we do need to work on you becoming a better warrior. And of course, we need to get you another sword. Maybe you will get another shot at those slimy beasts soon."

"But not now. We have a banquet prepared in your honor so the entire Kingdom can see you in all your splendor. Sir Yeled, the prince and heir to the throne. Oh yes, but before the grand banquet, my formerly hygienic son, you really do need a long hot bath."

The King kissed Yeled on both cheeks and then hugged him again. Yeled's heart was filled with such joy, such relief and such a feeling of being enough—more than he could ever remember feeling. He was the prince, the beloved of the King, lipnay melek at last.

The warriors' voices rang out with the tri-part acclamation reserved for great victors after great victories. "Huzzah for Sir Yeled. Huzzah, huzzah!"

"Let it be known and proclaimed," said the Royal Steward. "This Great King loves unlikely princes and princesses. That's all there is. In his presence, they become great. They become mishpat and tzedakah."

26

Dr. Ben

"Well, there's a little more," said Ben with his patented grin. "A bit of a shameless cliffhanger to draw people into the next book in the series. But let me stop there. In my little tale, all the prince ever needed was need. All he needed to do was run to the King's arms and look up into his loving, adoring eyes. Then, he would finally know beyond comprehension the love he had been missing and longing for. No quest was necessary. All he needed was to look up."

"Harvey, may I ask…Are you a man of faith?"

"Yes, of course. I am a member of First Church, just down the road, past the campus gates."

"Yes, let me be clearer. Are you a man of faith?"

"Not sure what you mean."

"When you look up into the eyes of your Da in Heaven, do you feel His love toward you—really? Do you feel honored beyond what you have earned or think you deserve? Do you feel adored as you are? Or is church just a collection of dogma and confessions to you? How long has it been since you have heard Him tell you, 'Well done, good and faithful servant? Or 'This is my beloved son with whom I am well pleased!'"

At that moment, the penny dropped—so they say. Harvey understood or at least saw that he was on the edge of a surprisingly vast shore of new understanding, deep and wide. He put his hands on his forehead as if to keep his brain from exploding and uttered far too loudly for the small space where they were seated, a variety of expletives I will not repeat in this book.

"I can't believe it. I came here today to find out if I completed my quest. Oh my gosh… it turns out I have been on the wrong quest. I am the prince. I pursued a quest instead of God's gaze—without even knowing it. I have spent my life ignoring God. What is wrong with me?"

"Exactly right," said Ben, grinning ear to ear. "All that is so true, great prince. Now that I have your attention, may I remind you of the good news of Christ in simple, non-church terms? You already know it. Sometimes we make it so elevated and theological that no one can make any sense of it. You must ask, child of God, that is it. All you need is need. Most of the time, you, like the prince, have been flailing around in your self-sufficiency and drive—mainly subconscious—nevertheless habitual, already baked into the cake, so they say. You must stop and recognize your need. Quests, real quests, bring us to that dangerous, vulnerable, and exposed place. Ask, and it shall be given to you.' The Apostle James agrees, 'You have not because you ask not.'"

By now, Harvey was in tears—not sad, but joyful. "Doc, I get it. I need this. I needed it forty years ago. Can I ask you a question? It is the businessman in me coming out. It seems to me every Christian leader should read your little book. I can't imagine I am alone. How do you get the word out?"

"You are so kind, my boy. My strategy is pretty simple, clever really, if I say so myself. Business leaders have many books; their shelves are littered with them. Some they have read, others not. Truthfully, they are a bit cynical about the ultimate helpfulness of books, old and new."

"Harvey, would you have read a book handed to you, even from a friend, and they said, 'This book is just the thing you need to change your life?' Would you have read it? No, me neither."

"On the other hand, leaders are curious about what their wives or husbands are reading. My strategy has been to get this little tale into the hands of the spouses of great leaders. It is almost a certainty they will pick it up sooner or later. Such is the nature of great princes and princesses. They can be such snoops," said Dr. McClellan, grinning a big toothy grin.

"Good plan," Harvey thought to himself. "An excellent plan!"

27

AND THEY ALL LIVED HAPPILY EVER AFTER?

So, all educated readers, and you certainly fit into that category, want to know how things turn out for any great tale's protagonist.

First, how did things turn out for the great prince? Silly. The prince is made-up, a fictional character. Undoubtedly, you have better things to do than to cause one of your hairs to go grey worrying over the fate of a make-believe person.

Ah, but what about Harvey? Did God, the Great King, make his business turn around? Did he have an advent, a unique vision from God leading to a new strategy that transformed his company? Did he rehire all the laid-off employees and develop a brilliant exit strategy allowing Harvey to play as much golf as he wanted?

Of course not. Great princes and princesses are rarely separated from great quests—or great battles, for that matter. The Kingdom is never conflict-free, and many conflicts can be horrible, often vast and complicated—so the need for more great princes and princesses who depend upon the Great King. The point of such tales is that great princes, who recognize their dependence on the Great King, respond in great battles differently than lesser princes.

Why? They don't need significance, security, and belonging to come from winning or losing—at least, not as much.

Please don't mistake my point. Great princes who dwell under the gaze of the Great King can be very competitive—they just don't need to be. They can be very aggressive on the battlefield—they don't need to be as much. They can even lose and sometimes fall short of their great lofty goals. It just doesn't affect them the way it does lesser princes.

Do they do excellence? Many business gurus focus on the importance and, in fact, Christ-likeness of doing excellence. Excellence is a great thing—dare I say, excellent? Great princes love excellence.

Yet, unlike lesser princes, they have come to see excellence is relative. The only absolute excellence—true excellence—occurred 2000 years ago. That once-for-all-time excellence earned great princes and princesses all that such excellent excellence is due.

Great princes now realize that the Great King is not impressed by any excellence they may achieve in their own power or will. No more excellence can gain one iota more of the Great King's blessing, favor, love, adoration, or the like. Lesser princes still hope to earn tidbits of the King's favor and blessings by ramping up their self-produced "excellence."

"Not so," says the Great King.

Great princes and princesses also know this is not an excuse to act like dullard trolls. Great princes, filled with the Spirit of the True Prince, want to do excellence. It is the Spirit of the Great Prince that makes it so.

Watch out for such great princes and princesses on the battlefield. They can be dominant warriors, hard fighters, and, more often than not, winners—they just don't have to be.

Here's what C.S. Lewis said in Mere Christianity.

> "What Satan put into the heads of our remote ancestors was the idea that they could 'be like gods'—could set up on their own as if they had created themselves—be their own masters—invent some sort of happiness for themselves outside of God, apart from God. And out of that hopeless attempt has come nearly all that we call human history—money, poverty, ambition, war, prostitution, classes, empires, slavery—the long terrible story of man trying to find something other than God which will make him happy. The reason why it can never succeed is this. God made us: invented us as a man invents an engine. A car is made to run on petrol, and it would not run properly on anything else. Now God designed the human machine to run on Himself. He Himself is the fuel our spirits were designed to burn, or the food our spirits were designed to feed on. There is no other. That is why it is just no good asking God to make us happy in our own way without bothering about religion. God cannot give us a happiness and peace apart from Himself because it is not there. There is no such thing." C.S. Lewis

Harvey gets it at last. He is learning to depend upon the gaze of his Great King. He is gradually embracing and asking for more and more of the Spirit of the True Prince within him, a change that is becoming more evident.

Ask Eleanor. After she came home—and cleaned up the obvious stain on her favorite Persian rug—she noticed Harvey took the browbeating better than he had in the past. There was probably a lot of other stuff igniting her rage. She had been quite irritated at him for some time.

A couple of days later, she wondered what got into Harvey. She noted he was calmer, more curious, creative, and a little more interested in her life. Yes, not perfect, but there had been a bit of a shift—noticeable. What caused her to truly wonder was that Harvey smiled more.

Harvey now regularly attends church and even asks many questions. He still feels out-of-sync with the organized church, but for wholly different reasons.

One thing hadn't changed. Harvey still couldn't sing. Eleanor cringed when the worship leader at church said, "All rise and sing Hymn number…" Don't get me wrong; she appreciated his new interest in singing and the new enthusiasm, yet she was worried the city might propose a new ordinance banning Harvey's voice as a public hazard, a nuisance, and bad for tourism in general. Whatever got into Harvey, it didn't affect his tin ear.

This topic was studied by a large not-for-profit research fellowship with far too much money to spend on such frivolous things. It turns out that only 26.8% of great princes can carry a tune (margin of error +/-2%). Harvey's voice would clearly be at the lowest extreme of that quartile. According to the same study, based upon a random sample of 200 great princes, 87% (margin of error

+/- 2%) would sing anyway if they wanted to. It was their sovereign right to be sure.

Harvey's business? Over the next few weeks, two larger assembly lines were shut down, a third redesigned to handle smaller jobs, and another twenty employees were laid off—but it was done fairly, as fairly as could be, with gracious severances—all in sync with Rotary's Four Way Test–at least as much as possible. Dwayne remained fired, of course.

Based on Scooter's advice, Harvey hired a professional exit planner who gave him ideas about what his company should do moving forward. For the first time in his life, he felt that he could begin a new quest and was excited about it.

They determined that negotiating a management team buyout was the best way to honor his current employees and to ensure sustainability. The proposed management team included Sadie as the new CEO, Sebastian over sales and marketing, and longtime employee Kyle Schatz in charge of operations.

After a thorough vetting of the three potential owners, the exit planner agreed that this team was both capable and committed long term—an ideal situation.

There was no one else in the world that Harvey trusted more than Sadie. When she brought a certified valuation of the business to the table, he saw little need for negotiation. She tossed out a number that she believed the company was worth on paper. Harvey concurred with a big smile on his face.

The management team buyout package involved an SBA loan, a promissory note, and a necessary commitment from Harvey that he would remain on contract for one year to mentor the new ownership team and assure major customers that the transition maintained the high levels of quality and service that Harvey's company had always been known for.

Sadie was sad to see Harvey leave but had to admit she was thrilled at the new challenge.

When all was completed, the employees gathered together in the largest warehouse for a grand celebration. Harvey, with Eleanor happily by his side, proposed a toast in honor of the new owners. Raising a plastic glass of Wild Turkey 101, he proclaimed, "I am so proud of the new owners and am confident they will accomplish far more than I ever have." He choked up a bit and wiped away a tear. "I wish my dad were here to see this. But I know, wherever he is, he is smiling."

Harvey is sleeping better—a little, anyway. Eleanor had the carpet professionally cleaned. Not a surprise to Harvey. She absolutely loved the Tale of the Unlikely Prince and has already started to read the second book in the Kingdom Quest trilogy. Harvey still reads Patterson novels, but now it's just because he wants to. And who doesn't?

Can't Forgive the Unforgivable?

The ForgIvIng Path is a unique confidential on-line 'live' learning experience that has helped 1000S of Christians forgive those deep wounds, hurts, betrayals and crimes using a time-tested biblical approach. The journey only takes a couple of hours and you will see the results immediately. See comments and actual results at www.forgivingpath.com now.

"Helped me to start releasing heavy burdens that were weighing my heart down. It made me realize that God really does love me. Being a survivor of much trauma and abuse, I was still holding onto a belief that I was being punished for something that I had done. I believed others deserved good but had a hard time believing that I too deserved good and was worthy."

"I think I have forgiven. Is that what you do here?"

On-line "live" Teaching Resource for Christian Parents

Good Enough Parent

"Good Enough Parent 1 & 2 are on-line teaching programs for parents that combine the Gospel with the latest from Neuroscience and Attachment Theory. Watch the intro video at www.goodenoughparent.online.

- "My child isn't isolating as much. I am more relaxed as a parent and asking God to direct my words with my child."
- "I really appreciated the non-shaming approach Dr. Senyard took to this information."
- "This whole program was exactly what I needed. The most beneficial reminder was that I just need to get 30% right to be a good enough parent."

goodenoughparent.online

Insightful and Transforming Biblical Historic Fiction

These are the long-lost journals of the Apostle Matthew. He and a colorful team of men and women followed the dangerous missionary charge of Jesus to go into all the world—in their case, Ethiopia—and preach the Gospel. Matthew's team was a striking testimony to the saving grace of their Lord. There was a former prostitute, a recovering opium addict, a shamed African princess, a freed Roman slave, and even a former member of the Sanhedrin who was present that evening Jesus was condemned to die.

"The Rabboni is a captivating journey through history, offering a compelling blend of biblical scholarship and storytelling that will resonate very well with readers interested in the early Christian era." Award Winning Author, K.C. Finn

Fresh Inspirational Women's Devotional

Dance is a fresh and timely look at seven of the most often overlooked, underappreciated, and misunderstood women in the Old Testament, written for individual and small group studies.

- Did you know there was a woman who almost single-handedly saved the line of Jesus? Her story reads like a Mission Impossible thriller.
- One woman snatched her city from a rampaging general, keeping David's fragile kingdom from splintering further.

"Dance is a powerful piece of writing that will motivate readers to reanalyze the role of the neglected women of biblical times. This book will become one of the prime selections in the canon of religious literature." Z. Sheikh, Reader's Favorite Reviewer.

ALSO BY DR. BILL SENYARD

Exciting and Fun Fantasy for Young and Old Readers

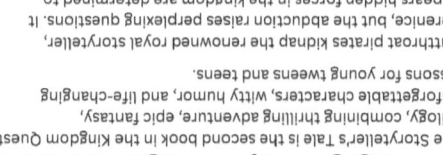

Inspired by C.S. Lewis' Chronicles of Narnia. 18-year-old 'unlikely' Prince Yeled wanted to finally prove to his adoptive father that he was worthy of being the prince heir. But what could he possibly do? He asks for a quest—no, a great quest—no, a heroically astonishing quest—challenging enough to prove his enoughness and finally earn the King's respect and love. Yeled will learn through thrilling, quirky, and sometimes unbelievable twists and turns that not all quests are what they might seem, and more importantly, this King is definitely not what he appears.

"Chronicles meets Princess Bride."

"Life Changing" Fantasy for Young Readers and Adults!

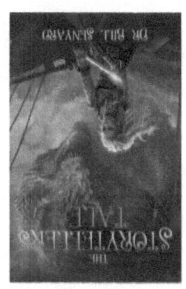

The Storyteller's Tale is the second book in the Kingdom Quest Trilogy, combining thrilling adventure, epic fantasy, unforgettable characters, witty humor, and life-changing lessons for young tweens and teens.

Cutthroat pirates kidnap the renowned royal storyteller, Berenice, but the abduction raises perplexing questions. It appears hidden forces in the kingdom are determined to expose her long-kept, dark secrets. What—or who—is driving this dangerous game? At what cost? Is it revenge? Punishment? Or something even more frightening? Remember, not all quests are alike...and this King is definitely not what he appears.

ENJOYING THIS BOOK?

I greatly appreciate you taking the time to read my book. It means a lot and I hope I am making a difference in your walk with Christ. If you have 60 seconds, it would mean a great deal to me if you could leave a short review on Amazon. It does wonders for the book and I love hearing how you benefited from it.

To leave your feedback:

1. Open your camera app.
2. Point your mobile device at the QR code below.
3. The Amazon review page will appear in your web browser.
4. Go down to "Review This Product" near the bottom of the page.
5. Thanks!

THE LAST QUEST

www.ingramcontent.com/pod-product-compliance
Lightning Source LLC
Chambersburg PA
CBHW030331010526
44119CB00036B/459/J